# lonely planet

# POCKET
# VANCOUVER

**Bianca Bujan**

# Contents

## Plan Your Trip — 4

The Journey Begins Here — 4
Our Picks — 6
Perfect Days — 16
Get Prepared — 20
When to Go — 22
Getting There — 24
Getting Around — 25
A Few Surprises — 28

Top: Canada Place (p44)
Bottom: Festival of Lights (p22), English Bay

# POCKET VANCOUVER

## Explore Vancouver 31

| | |
|---|---|
| Downtown & West End | 33 |
| Gastown & Chinatown | 53 |
| Yaletown & Granville Island | 69 |
| Main St & Mt Pleasant | 85 |
| Fairview & South Granville | 97 |
| Kitsilano & UBC | 109 |
| North Shore | 129 |

## Vancouver Toolkit 145

| | |
|---|---|
| Family Travel | 146 |
| Accommodations | 147 |
| Food, Drink & Nightlife | 148 |
| LGBTIQ+ Travelers | 150 |
| Health & Safe Travel | 151 |
| Responsible Travel | 152 |
| Accessible Travel | 154 |
| Nuts & Bolts | 155 |

## Land Acknowledgment

Lonely Planet respectfully acknowledges that Canada is the traditional territory of more than 630 First Nations communities as well as Inuit and Métis communities. We offer gratitude to the Indigenous Peoples for their care for, and teachings about, this land.

## ★ Top Experiences

| | |
|---|---|
| Stanley Park | 36 |
| Vancouver Art Gallery | 40 |
| West Coast Whale Watching | 50 |
| Gastown Steam Clock | 55 |
| Dr Sun Yat-Sen Classical Chinese Garden | 56 |
| Granville Island Public Market | 72 |
| Science World | 87 |
| VanDusen Botanical Garden | 100 |
| Museum of Anthropology | 112 |
| Worth a Trip: Richmond | 124 |
| Capilano Suspension Bridge | 132 |
| Grouse Mountain | 133 |
| Worth a Trip: Whistler | 140 |

PLAN YOUR TRIP

# The Journey Begins Here

People come to Vancouver for natural beauty: stunning seascapes, majestic mountains and towering trees frame the coastal city, where you can cycle, shop, ski and swim – all in one day, if you time it right. But Vancouver is more than just good looks. Its culinary and cultural offerings are as diverse as the neighborhoods that give the city its unique charm, while a melange of urban dwellers and outdoor daredevils add character. Vancouver is so friendly, flourishing and fabulous, you might just decide to stay.

**Bianca Bujan**
@bitsofbee
Born and raised in Vancouver, Bianca is an award-winning travel and food writer who loves to share the best things to see, do and eat in her home city. She's written several guidebooks for Lonely Planet, as well as stories for *National Geographic, Food & Wine, Travel + Leisure* and other publications.

**Cliffwalk, Capilano Suspension Bridge (p132)**
RONNIE CHUA/GETTY IMAGES

THE BEST

# Outdoor Adventures

Vancouver's variety of outdoor activities is the biggest draw; it's packed with beautiful beaches, forested hiking and biking trails, endless paddling and water sports, and spectacular local ski hills.

Ride a gondola up **Grouse Mountain**, the 'Peak of Vancouver' for summer and winter outdoor action. (pictured above; p133)

Hike **Quarry Rock**, known for its stunning forested trail with wooden steps and gravel pathways unveiling beautiful Burrard Inlet views at its final lookout point. (pictured above; p136)

Trek to **Whistler Blackcomb**, North America's largest ski resort, for endless alpine adventure, enjoyed year-round. (p140)

Cycle **Stanley Park seawall**, Vancouver's top outdoor hangout framing the perimeter of Stanley Park. (p36)

Tiptoe across **Capilano Suspension Bridge**, a memorably vertiginous experience above the Capilano River since 1889. (p132)

Right: Stanley Park seawall (p36)

FROM LEFT: OASISAMUEL/SHUTTERSTOCK, JAU-CHENG LIOU/SHUTTERSTOCK, MAX LINDENTHALER/SHUTTERSTOCK

## THE BEST

# Garden & Park Experiences

From one of North America's largest urban parks to the first Chinese 'scholars' garden' to be built outside Asia, Vancouver bursts with blooms coloring gardens and parks all over the city.

Stroll through **Stanley Park**, revered for its dramatic forest-and-mountain oceanfront views, beautiful beaches and dining. (pictured above; p36)

Find serenity in an urban landscape in the traditional **Dr Sun Yat-Sen Classical Chinese Garden**. (p56)

Smell flowers at **VanDusen Botanical Garden**, a plant lover's paradise with leafy walkways lined in local and exotic flora. (p100)

Check out **Queen Elizabeth Park**, the city's highest point offering panoramic views of mountain-framed skyscrapers downtown. (p104)

Nip into **Nitobe Memorial Garden**, a Japanese garden paying tribute to one man's lifelong dedication to fostering cross-cultural understanding. (pictured above; p115)

FROM LEFT: WIRESTOCK CREATORS/SHUTTERSTOCK, BOB POOL/SHUTTERSTOCK

### THE BEST
# Culinary Experiences

Global cuisine is a highlight here, with award-winning chefs serving up flavors from around the world. Fresh-catch seafood shines, and locally sourced farm-to-table food has put Vancouver on the Michelin map.

Eat your way around the **Granville Island Public Market** on a local-led tasting tour – a leisurely stroll that hits all the best spots. (pictured above; p72)

Feast along Mount Pleasant's **'Michelin Mile'**, a stretch known for its concentration of acclaimed restaurants that runs along Main Street. (p90)

Dine at **Salmon n' Bannock**, Vancouver's only Indigenous restaurant featuring fresh fish and locally sourced ingredients. (p105)

Grab a dog at **Japadog**, a Japanese take on the traditional hot dog and an iconic Vancouver food stop. The *kurobuta terimayo* is a Japadog fan favorite. (pictured above; p46)

Sample the best bites and bevies from around the globe at the **Richmond Night Market**, the largest of its kind in North America. (p124)

FROM LEFT: JEFF WHYTE/SHUTTERSTOCK, FELIX CHOO/ALAMY

THE BEST

# Famous Landmark Experiences

Be sure to bring your camera because Vancouver is packed with numerous architectural sites and historical points of interest that are must-sees during your visit to the city.

On the cobblestoned streets of historic Gastown, catch the 'hood's **Steam Clock** in action. (p55)

---

See sail-shaped **Canada Place**, the area's original convention-centre building, and stroll along a path of colored glass on the Canadian Trail. (p44)

---

Take in transport- and maritime-themed flourishes decorating the **Marine Building**, then nip inside and gawk at its palatial lobby. (pictured above; p45)

Explore beyond books at **Vancouver Public Library**, a Colosseum-like building with public rooftop garden and cityscape views. (pictured above; p43)

---

Snap a photo of the tripod-like **Olympic Cauldron**, a city landmark on Jack Poole Plaza and a permanent reminder of Vancouver's 2010 Winter Olympics. (p43)

FROM LEFT: FELIX LIPOV/SHUTTERSTOCK, JEFF WHYTE/SHUTTERSTOCK

Stanley Theatre (p104)

**THE BEST**

# Arts Experiences

The arts are everywhere in Vancouver, with galleries, shops and street-side displays showcasing the city's diversity. Consider a dance or theater performance, should you wish to see a show.

Visit **Vancouver Art Gallery**, host to blockbuster art shows and a striking contemporary collection. (p40)

---

Admire one of Canada's finest, most important collections of Northwest Coast aboriginal art and artifacts at the **Museum of Anthropology**. (p112)

---

See a live show at the **Stanley Theatre**, an art deco–style heritage theater. (p104)

Browse works of hailed Haida artist Bill Reid at the **Bill Reid Gallery of Northwest Coast Art**, Canada's only public art gallery of its kind. (p44)

---

Celebrate the Chinese-Canadian community and their contributions to Vancouver history and heritage at the **Chinese-Canadian Museum**. (p62)

## THE BEST

# Cultural Experiences

Learn about the region's Indigenous roots through tours and experiences, and discover the city's hidden cultural histories on engaging walking tours.

Discover Vancouver's rich yet often overlooked Black history on a walking tour along **Hogan's Alley**. (p61)

See a showcase of Vancouver's Chinese-Canadian history at the **Chinatown Storytelling Centre**. (pictured above; p60)

Get the full story of Stanley Park's past and present on an Indigenous-led guided park walk with **Talaysay Tours**. (p36)

Immerse yourself in Indigenous culture through historical stories and cultural works at the **Squamish Lil'wat Cultural Centre**, a shared showcase of the Squamish Nation and Lil'wat Nation. (p141)

Stroll through towering totem poles and galleries full of artifacts from around the world at the **Museum of Anthropology**. (pictured above; p112)

**Right: Squamish Lil'wat Cultural Centre (p141)**

## THE BEST

# Water & Wildlife Experiences

As a city surrounded by the ocean, mountains and trees, Vancouver teems with opportunities to adventure on the water or spot animals in the wild – from whales and seals, to bears and eagles.

Go **whale watching** from Granville Island. Spot orcas (killer whales), humpbacks, and grey whales, plus seals, sea lions and seabirds. (p50)

See the city from the water aboard **Aquabus**, a mini pedestrian ferry that connects Granville Island to several locations around town. (pictured above; p72)

Paddle through the sheltered waters of Deep Cove – sign up for a lesson or tour at the **Deep Cove Kayak Centre**. Stand-up paddle boarding is popular. (p136)

See birds at the **Bloedel Conservatory**, a delightful destination on a rainy day. Here you'll find tropical trees and plants bristling with hundreds of free-flying birds. (pictured above; p104)

Meet farm animals at **Maplewood Farm**, a family-owned farmstead found on Vancouver's North Shore. (p137)

FROM LEFT: RONNIE CHUA/SHUTTERSTOCK, WIRESTOCK/GETTY IMAGES

# Best for Kids

Shop and play at **Kids Market**, a multi-level mall packed with wooden toys, well-curated books, a magic shop and play space. (p78)

Connect with coastal aquatic life at **Vancouver Aquarium**, Canada's largest. Observe more than 65,000 animals here, watch special shows and run wild in interactive play spaces. (p44)

Find fun inside domed **Science World**, a multi-level mash-up of activities and exhibits that makes science exciting for little ones (and grown ups too). (p87)

Take flight with **FlyOver Canada**, a thrilling flight-simulation ride that whisks you off on a virtual trip through some of Canada's most beautiful natural sights. (p44)

Spray, splash and slide at the **Granville Island Water Park**, the largest free outdoor water park of its kind in North America. (p79)

# Best for Free

Spend the day at **Second Beach**, a family-friendly area in Stanley Park with a grassy playground and huge outdoor swimming pool. (p37)

View Vancouver's 300+ vibrant **Metropolitan Murals**. The street art is a lasting cultural legacy of the now-closed Vancouver Mural Festival. (p88)

Play outside at **Creekside Park**, home to Vancouver's largest playground with a zipline, wooden climbing tower, swings, water and sand play areas. (p90)

Snap photos of **Engine 374**, the historic locomotive that pulled the first transcontinental passenger train into Vancouver to link the country from coast to coast by train. (p78)

Learn about local flora and wildlife in Stanley Park's charming nature center **Nature House**. (p37)

# Perfect Days

Whether you want to play outside, admire art, eat your way around the city's best restaurants or just relax and take it all in, these itineraries will help you get started.

**Granville Island Public Market (p72)**

### DAY ONE

## Only Have One Day?

**MORNING**

Get up early and cycle around **Stanley Park** (p36). Admire the park's towering totem poles, unearth nature in the **Lost Lagoon** (p37) and look for the **Girl in Wetsuit** (pictured above; p39) statue.

**AFTERNOON**

Dine alfresco at **1931 Gallery Bistro** (p41) before embarking on a downtown gallery tour. Peruse paintings at the **Vancouver Art Gallery** (p40), then head to the **Bill Reid Gallery of Northwest Coast Art** (p44) to admire works by the city's hailed Haida artist.

**EVENING**

Cocktails and live music at the Fairmont Pacific Rim hotel are top-notch – and the perfect opener to dinner afterwards in its upstairs restaurant **Botanist** (p47). Expect a seasonal Canadian feast.

### DAY TWO
## A Weekend Trip

#### MORNING
Bask in the blooms at **VanDusen Botanical Garden** (pictured above; p100) and look for local wildlife as you meander around the mirror-calm lake. If you're feeling snacky, enjoy a coffee and treat at the **Garden Cafe** (p101). Then pop into the domed **Bloedel Conservatory** (p104) to see exotic birds and butterflies.

#### AFTERNOON
Hit the stretch of stylish shops along South Granville. Pick up some keepsakes from **Pacific Arts Market** (p107) while you're there, and take home some sweet treats from **Purdy's Chocolates** (p107).

#### EVENING
Head to Granville Island and snack your way through its **Public Market** (p72) before catching the sunset with brews and views on the patio at **Tap & Barrel Bridges** (p51).

### DAY THREE
## A Short Break

#### MORNING
Get up early and head to West 4th Avenue in Kitsilano. Start with breakfast at **Sophie's Cosmic Cafe** (p120) or **Jam Cafe** (p120; be prepared for a possible wait), and then browse the shops along the strip.

#### AFTERNOON
Shop your way along the West 4th strip, popping into shops like **Old Faithful** (p123), **Zulu Records** (pictured above; p123) and **Pacific Boarder** (p123). If it's a sunny day, stroll down to **Kitsilano Beach** (p118). If you need to cool off, take a dip in the ocean or **Kitsilano Pool** (p117) while you're there.

#### EVENING
Make your way to **Maenam** (p121) at the corner of 4th & Burrard for some of the city's best Thai food. Be sure to order a drink from their creative cocktail list.

# If You Have More Time

Start with a stroll along the cobblestone streets of historic Gastown; snap a photo of the **Steam Clock** (p55) before browsing the Water St shops, including **Herschel Supply Co** (p67) and **John Fluevog Shoes** (p67). Consider a late-morning brunch at **Water St Cafe** (p65; book ahead), in a 1906 heritage building.

Chinatown is right next door. Explore Vancouver's Chinese-Canadian history through immersive exhibits at the **Chinatown Storytelling Centre** (p60), or pop across the street to the **Chinese-Canadian Museum** (p62) to learn about the Chinese-Canadian community that made an impact on Vancouver's heritage. Head outdoors next for a guided tour in the tranquil **Dr Sun Yat-Sen Classical Chinese Garden** (p56), ending with a cup of complimentary tea.

Wrap up your day with pre-dinner drinks at **Laowai** (p66) speakeasy or **Keefer Bar** (p66), then head over to local legend **Phnom Penh** (p64) for Cambodian and Vietnamese comfort foods. We recommend ordering the wings.

**Water St, Gastown (p78)**

## A City Day Trip

Hop aboard SeaBus (pictured above) and spend the day on the other side of the water, exploring the **Shipyards District** and **Lower Lonsdale** (p134) on Vancouver's North Shore.

---

First, pop into the shops at the Lonsdale Quay. Then peruse the paintings at the **Polygon Gallery** (p135) before catching the Lonsdale StreetCar – a free electric shuttle, which will take you around the Lower Lonsdale area. Check out **Hunter & Hare** (p135), then walk back down to the water.

---

Snag a spot on the sunsoaked patio of **King Taps** (p135), or opt for a nicer dinner indoors at **Pier 7** (p139). Both are great sunset spots before catching a Seabus back to the city.

## On a Rainy Day

Start your day with a galavant through the city's iconic geodesic dome **Science World** (p87). Then stroll up Main St on a self-guided tour of street art decorating side streets with Vancouver's metropolitan murals (bring an umbrella).

---

Explore cool boutiques around the Main St and Broadway intersection, including vintage fave **Mintage Mall** (p95) and **Turnabout Luxury Resale** (p95). Continue up Main St to shop Vancouver's best indie stores, from vinyl-loving **Neptoon Records** (p94) to quirky **Regional Assembly of Text** (pictured above; p95).

---

Wrap up your day with an early dinner, washed down with a creative cocktail, at vibrant Vietnamese hot spot **Anh & Chi** (p92).

# Get Prepared

### BOOK AHEAD

**Three months before**
Book summer-season hotel stays and tickets for sought-after shows, festivals and live performances.

**One month before**
Book car rental and reserve tables at any top restaurants. Buy tickets for Vancouver Canucks and Vancouver Whitecaps games.

**One week before**
Check what local events are coming up on straight.com.

## Manners Matter

The cliché of the courteous Canadian is accurate. You'll hear 'sorry' frequently – and not only when someone's at fault. Don't be surprised if someone holds the door or greets you with a friendly 'Hello'. Use please and thank you in formal exchanges. Canadians are courteous, including as drivers on the road. Canadians are generally friendly and approachable.

## Cannabis in Canada

That's likely not a skunk you smell as you're strolling through the city. Cannabis is legal and widely available in Vancouver, with licensed shops throughout town. You'll probably catch its scent downtown or in parks – it's part of city life. Smoking is allowed in many outdoor spaces, though discretion is advised. Locals are unfazed, and curious tourists will find access easy. While cannabis is legal in Canada, it's still illegal to cross borders with it.

## Things to Know

**Drinking** Vancouver requires you to be 19 years of age to purchase, possess or consume alcohol. The government regulates alcohol, retailing and distributing alcoholic beverages throughout the city.

**Words** There are some common words you may not recognize here such as toque (a knitted hat usually worn in winter); two-four (a 24-pack of beer); freezies (ice pops); washroom (bathroom or restroom); clicks (used to refer to kilometers when driving); Canadian tuxedo (denim top and bottom); tobogganing (sledding in the snow); and there are many more.

**Metric System** Distance is measured in kilometers, gas is pumped in liters, and air temperature forecasts are Celsius. While many other countries do the same, it's a common assumption that Canada follows the same measurement system as its neighbors to the south.

## TIPPING

Tipping is common in Canada, especially when dining out or participating in a guided tour.

**20%**
**Restaurants & cocktail bars**

**$1–$2**
**Coffee shops & cafes (counter service)**

**10–15%**
**Taxis & rideshare**

**$5–$10**
**Hotel concierge & valet**

## DAILY BUDGET

### BUDGET: Less than $100

- Dorm bed: **$50**
- Food court meal: **$10**
- Pizza slice: **$4**
- Happy hour beer special: **$9**
- All-day transit pass: **$11.25**

### MIDRANGE: $100–300

- Double room in a standard hotel: **$200**
- Dinner for two: **$60 (excluding drinks)**
- Craft beer for two: **$20**
- Museum entry: **$15–25**

### TOP END: More than $300

- Four-star hotel room: **from $350**
- Fine-dining meal for two: **$100 (excl drinks)**
- Cocktails for two: **$28**
- Taxi trips around the city: **from $8**

**Currency**
Canadian dollar ($)

**Language**
English, French

**Time**
Pacific Time (GMT/UTC minus eight hours)

YUESTOCK/SHUTTERSTOCK

## CENT SAVER

Save money and skip lines with a **Vancouver Attractions Pass** *(vancouverattractions.com),* covering discounted entry to top spots like Capilano Suspension Bridge and the Aquarium when you buy them as a bundle.

**PLAN YOUR TRIP · GET PREPARED**

# When to Go

Any time is a good time to visit Vancouver. The city offers four seasons full of fun for everyone, indoors and out.

Vancouver or 'Raincouver' is known for its soggy skies due to its geographical location. Despite the wet weather, each season offers something special. Summer (June–August), considered peak season, brings packed beaches and fun on the water. Fall (September–November) colors the city in fall foliage while temperatures remain mild. Spring (March–May) brings cherry blossoms and leafy gardens, while winter (November–February) is for snow sports, with ski hills nearby and Whistler a car ride away.

## The Big Events

**May** **Vancouver International Children's Festival** is all about kids. As North America's first and longest-running professional performing arts festival for young audiences, it spotlights performing arts for children.

**June** Early summer brings the **Dragon Boat Festival**, North America's largest dragon boat race, set around False Creek, with cultural performances and family fun. Music lovers flock to the **Vancouver International Jazz Festival**, a mix of free and ticketed indoor and outdoor concerts.

**August** Vancouver's **Pride Parade** transforms the city into a vibrant celebration of the LGBTIQ+ community with a massive parade, performances and festivities along Davie Street and Sunset Beach.

**November/December** The festive season arrives with **Vancouver Christmas Market**, a European-style market at Jack Poole Plaza, with artisan goods,

### Vancouver Weather

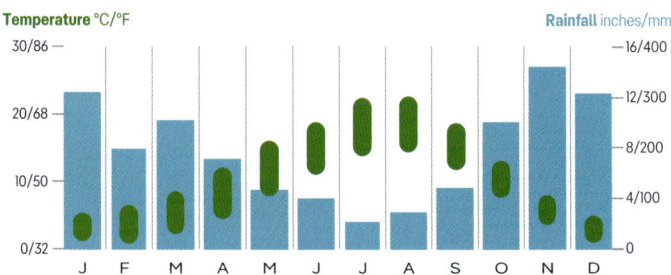

Vancouver Dragon Boat Festival

mulled wine and live music. The **Festival of Lights** turns VanDusen Botanical Garden into a glowing wonderland lit by more than a million twinkling bulbs – a holiday-must for garden lovers.

## Food & Flower Festivals

**January/February** The year starts with the **Dine Out Vancouver Festival**, offering set menus at 300+ restaurants offered for a reasonable price. Around the same time, the **Hot Chocolate Festival** sweetens the city with creative cocoa concoctions. Wine lovers enjoy tastings and seminars at the **Vancouver International Wine Festival**, one of North America's top wine events.

**March–July** Spring blossoms in various hues of pink with the **Vancouver Cherry Blossom Festival**, celebrating 40,000+ cherry blossom trees with walks, performances and ceremonies. Seasonal food events highlight BC's springtime bounty, including the **Spot Prawn Festival**, which comes to the city in May and July's **Steveston Salmon Festival**.

---

### ACCOMMODATION LOWDOWN

Summer and winter are the busiest seasons for visitors to Vancouver, and pricing reflects that, with spiked accommodation rates during those seasons. Early fall and late spring are great times to enjoy the milder weather and lower costs.

# ✈ Getting There

Most international and domestic visitors arrive by air at Vancouver International Airport (YVR) in Richmond. A few flights arrive at Abbotsford International Airport (YXX), further away.

## From Vancouver International Airport to the City Centre

### By SkyTrain
The Canada Line SkyTrain runs from Vancouver International Airport to downtown Vancouver, 13km north, in approximately 25 minutes. Trains depart regularly throughout the day. Buy tickets at machines in the terminal or via TransLink's mobile options (translink.ca). A one-way ticket is about $9; off-peak fares can be cheaper.

### By Taxi or Rideshare
A taxi from Vancouver International Airport to downtown Vancouver takes around 30 minutes, depending on traffic. Rideshare services like Uber and Lyft have three dedicated pickup points at the airport – follow the signs to locate them. The average cost is $30 to $50.

### By Car
Rental desks are inside the airport. Renting a car offers flexibility if you're heading beyond the city to Whistler or Vancouver Island. However, downtown parking is limited, metered and time-restricted. Most hotels charge parking fees.

## Other Points of Entry

### Pacific Central Station
Vancouver's main hub for long-distance train and bus travel. VIA Rail *(viarail.com)* trains arrive from across Canada; Amtrak *(amtrak.com)* services Seattle and destinations further south. Greyhound *(greyhound.com)* has routes from Seattle, and BC Connector *(bcconnector.com)* links Vancouver with Kelowna, Kamloops, Whistler and Victoria.

### Vancouver Cruise Terminal
Arrival point for travelers coming by sea from Alaska, Hawaii and the Pacific Coast. In downtown at Canada Place.

# Getting Around

If you're staying downtown, sightseeing in the city is simple by foot, bike, bus, ferry or boat. To venture further afield, you'll want wheels. Stretch your budget further by taking the bus, SkyTrain or a mini-ferry – public transportation makes it easy to explore without a car here.

## Bus

Vancouver has a safe and extensive public bus network that connects to six regions across Metro Vancouver. Most buses have bike racks, are wheelchair accessible and offer free wi-fi. The network spans three fare zones and runs from 5am to 1am in central areas.

## SkyTrain

The SkyTrain (pictured right) is a fast, accessible way to reach downtown from the airport or explore outer regions. Three lines serve different areas: the Expo Line (downtown to Burnaby, New West, Surrey), Canada Line (to YVR Airport and Richmond) and Millennium Line (Vancouver to Coquitlam).

## SeaBus

This passenger-only ferry connects downtown Vancouver to the North Shore in just 12 minutes. It arrives at Lonsdale Quay in Lower Lonsdale, with access to North Vancouver's trails and ski hills. A nearby bus loop links to further destinations.

## Car Rental

Rentals are available at the airport and across the city. Use **DriveBC**

FROM LEFT: HAND-ROBOT/GETTY IMAGES, LAWRENCE WORCESTER/LONELY PLANET

--- **ESSENTIAL APP** ---
Visit the official TransLink site for schedules at translink.ca, or download the Transit App.

*(drivebc.ca)* for route planning and traffic updates. Downtown parking can be expensive. Locate spots and pay with **EasyPark** *(easypark.ca)*.

### RideShare & Taxi
Uber and Lyft operate in Vancouver, along with taxis from companies like Yellow Cab, Vancouver Taxi and Black Top & Checker Cabs.

### Bike
With 300km of bike routes and dedicated lanes, biking is a low-cost, safe travel option. Use **Bike Hub** *(bikehub.ca)* for planning. **Mobi** *(mobibikes.ca)* offers bike sharing. Rentals are available near Stanley Park and Granville Island, which provides free bike-valet service.

### Miniferry
Mini passenger ferries like **Aqua-Bus** *(theaquabus.com)* and **False Creek Ferries** *(granvilleislandferries.bc.ca)* connect Granville Island and False Creek. They are bike- and wheelchair-friendly.

### Float Plane
Connecting to the coast is quick by air. **Harbour Air** *(harbourair.com)* is a passenger-only float plane connecting to Vancouver Island, the Sunshine Coast, even Whistler and Seattle from downtown Vancouver. It offers flight-seeing tours too.

---

## Public Transport Essentials

### Trip Planning
TransLink operates Vancouver's public transit system, including buses, SkyTrain and SeaBus. Fares are based on service type, zone and time of day.

Along with trip-planning resources, the **TransLink** website *(translink.ca)* has a comprehensive section on fares and passes covering its combined bus, SeaBus and SkyTrain services. It also includes information and route maps for cyclists traveling by bike and public transit.

### Buying Tickets
Exact change (or more) is required when buying bus tickets on board; buses use fare machines and change is not given. Tickets are valid for up to 90 minutes of transfer travel.

Buy single-use tickets and all-access day passes from vending machines at SeaBus and SkyTrain stations – tickets must be purchased before boarding (machines give change, and also accept debit and credit cards). Buy Compass Cards ($6 deposit) from these machines or at designated Compass retailers around the city, including London Drugs branches.

Children aged 12 and under ride for free.

## Cut Costs

The transit system is divided into three geographic zones. All bus trips are one-zone fares, irrespective of distance or zones travelled across. If you buy a stored-value Compass Card, fares are charged at a lower rate.

**TRAVEL COSTS**

**Adult SkyTrain fare**
$3.35

**Adult bus fare**
$3.35

**Adult miniferry fare**
$4.50

--- **COMPASS CARD** ---

Consider a reloadable Compass Card. Tap on and off at readers; reload online or in stations.

### TICKETS

| Ticket/Pass Type | Adult | Child (5–18yrs) |
|---|---|---|
| 1-zone | $3.35 | $2.10 |
| 2-zone | $4.55 | $3.10 |
| 3-zone | $6.20 | $4.25 |
| Day pass | $11.25 | $8.25 |
| Monthly pass (1-zone) | $104.90 | $59.95 |

### TICKET ZONES

- There are three fare zones.
- Buses always charge the one-zone fare.
- Weekdays after 6:30pm, weekends and holidays: the one-zone fare is charged system-wide.

# 🎁 A Few Surprises

If you look beyond the city's surface, you'll find lots of hidden surprises, from magic mini fairy doors to hidden gardens.

## Fairy Doors

Found tucked in the trees of Stanley Park and the artsy alleys by Dude Chilling Park, some little surprises can be spotted if you look closely. No bigger than a handspan, miniature fairy doors are tiny installations embedded in tree trunks, fence posts and curbs throughout the city. Blink and you might miss them, but stop to look closer and you might discover a small world behind the doors.

Each door is distinct. Some are brightly painted. Others are rustic and mossy, hinting at an entire fairy neighborhood hidden in plain sight. Whether designed to ignite a child's imagination or simply an artist's secret offering to the city, these doors add a layer of magic to your afternoon walk. They're neither marked not explained – just quietly waiting to be found. A map exists (if you really want to cheat), but the joy lies in the surprise.

## Concrete Canvases

Across Vancouver's neighborhoods – from the bohemian bustle of Commercial Drive to the tree-lined streets of the West End – drab utility boxes have evolved into decorative mini murals. Covered in color, bold patterns and abstract scenes, these concrete structures are now unexpected showcases of local art.

From sunflowers to surreal forest scenes, every painted box is a spontaneous surprise. They remind passersby that art doesn't have to be housed in a gallery. Instead, it can live alongside traffic lights and bike racks, catching your eye as you cross the street. These bright boxes definitely add another layer of creativity to the city.

---

**OFFBEAT VANCOUVER**

Uncover hidden Black history on a walking tour through Strathcona and **Hogan's Alley** (p61).

Find family fun at **Maplewood Farm** (p137), an urban farm tucked away on Vancouver's North Shore.

Forget Capilano Canyon. Teeter across the free, unsung suspension bridge in **Lynn Canyon Park** (p137).

Enjoy the most hidden and unusual green space on UBC campus at the **Asian Centre** (p115).

Multilingual street sign, Chinatown

## Park Pianos

During the summer months, music fills the air thanks to these surprising pop-ups – upright pianos, quietly positioned in city parks such as David Lam, Granville Island and Coal Harbour. There's no schedule – just the open invitation to sit and play. One day you might hear a child pounding out Chopsticks, another, a jazz musician entertaining a gathering crowd with skilled tunes. These park pianos are impromptu gathering spots: think public art you can literally play, and a testament to Vancouver's creative spontaneity.

## Multilingual Street Signs

Vancouver's street signs don't just tell you where you are; they also hint at where the city's residents have come from. In Chinatown, road signs include Chinese characters alongside English words, echoing generations of cultural connections. South of Punjabi Market, Gurmukhi script shares sidewalk space with English, signaling one of Canada's oldest south Asian neighborhoods.

Indigenous languages are reclaiming their rightful place with names like 'X̱wáýx̱way' (the original name of the Stanley Park area) appearing on trails in Stanley Park, and 'šxʷməθkʷəy̓əmasəm St' in Kitsilano. These signs aren't just for finding your way. They are time capsules indicating a land that holds many stories, in many voices.

# Explore Vancouver

| | |
|---|---|
| Downtown & West End | 33 |
| Gastown & Chinatown | 53 |
| Yaletown & Granville Island | 69 |
| Main St & Mt Pleasant | 85 |
| Fairview & South Granville | 97 |
| Kitsilano & UBC | 109 |
| North Shore | 129 |

**Worth a Trip**

| | |
|---|---|
| Richmond | 124 |
| Whistler | 140 |

**Vancouver's Walking Tours**

| | |
|---|---|
| Walk Downtown | 42 |
| Walk Chinatown | 58 |
| Granville Island Artisan Amble | 76 |
| Metropolitan Mural Meander | 88 |
| Walk South Granville | 102 |
| Walk UBC Campus & Gardens | 114 |
| Walk Lower Lonsdale | 134 |

**Vancouver Art Gallery (p40)**
LISSANDRA MELO/SHUTTERSTOCK

**See p46** for eating, drinking and shopping listings

# Explore
# Downtown & West End

At the heart of Vancouver lies a scenic peninsula bordered by the waters of the Pacific Ocean, naturally divided into three distinct areas. First is the dynamic downtown core, with its grid-patterned streets lined with upscale boutiques, diverse eateries, and shimmering glass towers that fan out from Granville Street and West Georgia. Nearby, the West End offers a quieter charm, with tree-lined side streets, mid-century apartment buildings and a vibrant LGBTQ+ community. Finally, there's Stanley Park, Canada's finest urban green space, packed with trails, beaches, wildlife and some of Vancouver's top attractions.

## Getting Around

### Walk
Downtown's grid-like streets are walkable and easy to navigate.

### Train
SkyTrain's Expo Line and Canada Line run throughout downtown.

### Bus
Bus #5 runs along Robson Street and connects to the West End, bus #6 connects with Davie Village and SkyTrain routes, and bus #19 goes through Stanley Park to downtown.

### Boat
SeaBus is a quick way to get to/from downtown from the North Shore.

### Car
There are multiple car parks and parking meters. Stanley Park has pay-and-display parking.

**Stanley Park seawall (p36)**
OLEG CHARYKOV/GETTY IMAGES

## THE BEST

**ART GALLERY** Vancouver Art Gallery (p40)

**GREEN SPACE** Stanley Park (p36)

**ICONIC LANDMARK** Canada Place (p44)

**INDIGENOUS ART** Bill Reid Gallery of Northwest Coast Art (p44)

**ANIMAL ENCOUNTERS** Vancouver Aquarium (p44)

## ★ TOP EXPERIENCE

# Stanley Park

One of North America's largest urban green spaces, Stanley Park is revered for its dramatic forest-and-mountain oceanfront views. But there's more to this 400-hectare woodland than good looks. The park is studded with nature-hugging trails, family-friendly attractions, sunset beaches and tasty places to eat.

MAP P34, **C1**

**PLANNING TIP**
Rent a bike and cycle the scenic seawall, one of the city's most popular cycling routes. It's walkable, too; count two to three hours on foot or an hour by bike.

Scan this QR code for a full map of the park's attractions.

### Seawall
Built between 1917 and 1980, the park's paved seawall is Vancouver's top outdoor hangout. Framing the park's perimeter, it offers spectacular waterfront and forest views. Along the way, the seawall hits several of the park's highlights. About 1.5km from the W Georgia St entrance, at **Brockton Point**, are brightly-painted totem poles and exquisitely-carved Coast Salish welcome arches honoring the area's original inhabitants. For the park's full story, past and present, consider an Indigenous-led guided park walk with **Talaysay Tours** *(talaysay.com/vancouver; adult/child $80/66).*

### Hollow Tree
In its early tourist destination days, a giant western red cedar was the park's top attraction. The tree's bottom section had a massive hollowed-out area where visitors would pose for photos, sometimes in their cars. The fragile structure still remains, and artist Douglas Coupland celebrates it with a latter-day golden replica near the city's Marine Drive Canada Line station.

## Natural Attractions

Stanley Park is studded with wildlife-watching spots. Start at **Lost Lagoon**, a nature sanctuary near the W Georgia St entrance. On its perimeter pathway, keep your eyes peeled for blue herons and wandering racoons. Plunging deeper into the park's more secluded trails, spot wrens, hummingbirds and chittering Douglas squirrels. If you come across a coyote, treat them with respect and give them space. For an introduction to the area's flora and fauna, start at **Stanley Park Nature House**, with friendly volunteers and exhibits on wildlife, history and ecology. It runs well-priced guided walks.

## Beaches & Views

The park is home to several sandy beaches. **Second Beach** is a family-friendly area on

**QUICK BREAK**
For a refined brunch in the park, try the **Teahouse in Stanley Park**. The burgers and beer are worth a stop at Stanley Park Brewing.

the western side with a grassy playground, an ice-cream-serving concession stand and outdoor swimming pool. It's also close to **Ceperley Meadows**, where free outdoor movies are screened in summer. For more tranquility, try **Third Beach**, a sandy stretch with plenty of logs to sit against – a favored summer-evening spot for Vancouverites.

Topping the list of popular park viewpoints is **Prospect Point**. One of Vancouver's best lookouts, this scenic spot is located at the park's northern tip. In summer you'll be edging in for elbow room with tour parties – head down the steep stairs to the viewing platform for more space. Stop at **Prospect Point Bar & Grill** for refreshments; aim for a deck table.

**Lost Lagoon (p37)**

### Statue Spotting

Stanley Park is home to a surprising assortment of statues. Look out for them as you make your way around the park. On the seawall, you'll easily spot **Girl in Wetsuit** in the water, a 1972 bronze by Elek Imredy. Harder to find is the **Robert Burns Memorial**, unveiled by British prime minister Ramsay MacDonald in 1928, and the dramatic bronze **Harry Jerome Statue** of the Canadian sprint legend who held six world records and won bronze at the 1964 Summer Olympics in Toyko. Near the Malkin Bowl, marking the first official visit of a US president to Canada in 1923, is the **President Harding Memorial**.

### For Kids

The **Vancouver Aquarium** (p44) is an obvious draw for kids, as is the outdoor **Second Beach Pool**, but there are some additional must-dos for those aged under 10. Check out the **Stanley Park Nature House**, or make a beeline for the waterfront waterpark near Lumberman's Arch; you'll find a big playground here too.

Before leaving the park, pay a visit to the man behind the name. Take the ramp running parallel with the seawall near the W Georgia St entrance to find the **Lord Stanley Statue**, arms outstretched, tucked in the trees. On the plaque are the words Lord Stanley used at the park's 1889 dedication ceremony: 'To the use and enjoyment of people of all colours, creeds and customs for all time.' It's a sentiment that still resonates loudly here today.

**THE POET OF STANLEY PARK**
The only person to be legally buried in Stanley Park is writer Pauline Johnson. A champion of Indigenous culture, she wrote a bestselling book on Coast Salish legends. When she died in 1913, thousands of locals lined the streets to mark her passing. Her memorial is a few steps from the seawall's Siwash Rock landmark.

## ★ TOP EXPERIENCE

# Vancouver Art Gallery

The **Vancouver Art Gallery** *(VAG; vanartgallery.bc.ca; adult/child $35/free)* is Western Canada's largest public art museum, where blockbuster international shows combine with striking contemporary collections. There are often three or four main exhibitions, but save time for the top-floor Emily Carr paintings, showcasing swirling nature-themed works by BC's favorite historic artist.

MAP P34 **G3**

### Gallery 101

Before you arrive, check online for details on the latest exhibitions; the biggest shows of the year are typically on display in summer. But this gallery isn't just about the blockbusters. Check out the other offerings found in this landmark building. Start on the top floor, where British Columbia's most famous painter is often showcased. Emily Carr (1871–1945) is celebrated for her swirling, nature-inspired paintings of regional landscapes and Indigenous culture. Watercolors were her main approach, and the gallery has a large collection of her works. The Gallery Store is one of the city's best spots to pick up art gifts, with a wide range of treasures to choose from.

### Join the Locals

The gallery isn't just a place to stare at cool art. Every few months, **FUSE** weekend socials transform the domed heritage building into a popular evening event with DJs, bars, live performances and quirky gallery tours. It's Vancouver's most popular adult-art party spot and a highlight of the city's art scene. Dress up and expect a clubby vibe enmeshed with engaging art displays.

**PLANNING TIP**
If you're on a budget, admission is free on the first Friday of every month during Free First Friday Nights from 4pm to 8pm. Admission is always free for visitors aged 18 and under.

Scan this QR code for a full list of exhibits and events.

STEPHANIE BRACONNIER/SHUTTERSTOCK

## Offsite

Just three blocks from Vancouver Art Gallery, between Thurlow and Bute Streets on West Georgia and tucked beneath the Shangri-La Hotel, **Offsite** is the gallery's dedicated outdoor public art space. Though modest in size, it delivers thought-provoking contemporary installations. Local and international artists are invited to engage with the site's urban context, producing works that respond to shifting social and cultural landscapes. Installed each spring and fall, these temporary art projects range from large-scale portraits to intricate models of historic local buildings. The result is a dynamic, ever-changing alfresco gallery that regularly stops people as they pass – often prompting spontaneous photos and curious reflection.

**QUICK BREAK**
The large patio of the on-site **1931 Gallery Bistro** is a great spot to grab a coffee and people-watch over Robson St. For a fancy dinner, chic Hawksworth is just steps away.

# 🚶 WALKING TOUR

# Walk Downtown

The heart of city-centre Vancouver is a grid of major streets lined with shops and restaurants. It's also home to galleries, historic buildings and an accessible rooftop garden overlooking shimmering glass towers. Take your time following this itinerary – it has plenty of pit-stop cafes and coffeeshops en route.

| START | END | LENGTH |
|---|---|---|
| Olympic Cauldron | Marine Building | 3km; one hour |

### 1 Olympic Photo Op

On Jack Poole Plaza, the tripod-like **Olympic Cauldron** is a city landmark and a reminder of Vancouver's 2010 Winter Olympics. Still lit occasionally, it's a great spot to snap photos framed by the grand backdrop of the North Shore mountains and Coal Harbour.

### 2 Public Art

One of Canada's largest convention centers hugs the waterfront with floor-to-ceiling windows. Follow the external walkway around **Convention Centre West Building** to admire giant public artworks, including a pixelated orca by Douglas Coupland and a bright-blue steel raindrop by German art collective Inges Idee. Views of Stanley Park are sweeping.

### 3 Architectural Icon

Next door is the area's original convention centre, sail-shaped Canada Place (p44). Stroll along the **Canadian Trail**, a pathway of colored glass representing Canada's 13 regions (10 provinces and three territories). It begins with an Indigenous art installation titled, *Salish Sea, the Journey Within*. Canada Place is also home to the cruise-ship port.

### 4 Lunch Stop

Inside a stately heritage building, **Vancouver Art Gallery** (p40) is a must-see (especially the top-floor Emily Carr paintings). Hungry? Dive into the nearby food trucks for an alfresco lunch.

### 5 Literary Landmark

There's more than books to check out at the Colosseum-like **Vancouver Public Library**. This is the home to several annual events, and a wide range of special collections. Ride the elevator to the ninth floor to access a large public garden with cityscape views.

### 6 Heritage Hotel

Nip into the lobby of **Fairmont Hotel Vancouver**, the city's grand-dame heritage hotel. Opened in 1939, it was built as a grand railway hotel, and has hosted famous guests such as Queen Elizabeth II. Look for 1930s design features and the two friendly dogs that call the concierge desk home.

### 7 Oldest Building

Historic **Christ Church Cathedral** seems out of place among the glass towers. This is downtown Vancouver's oldest surviving building, now a listed Class A heritage-listed building. Gaze at its stained-glass windows and eye-popping hammer-beam ceiling.

### 8 A 1930s Marvel

The spectacular **Marine Building** (p45) dates to the art deco era. Allow ample time to peruse its exterior transport- and maritime-themed decorative flourishes. Inside, gawk at its palatial lobby.

## EXPERIENCES

### Have Fun Under Five Sails  ARCHITECTURAL LANDMARK

The area's original convention-center building, sail-shaped **Canada Place** (MAP: ❶ P34 **H4**), is a top sight. Stroll its pier-like outer promenade and watch the floatplanes taking off from, and landing on, the water here. Take flight with **FlyOver Canada** (MAP: ❷ P34 **H3**; *flyovercanada.com; online/at gate $37/40*), a thrilling flight-simulation ride that takes you on a virtual trip through some of Canada's most beautiful natural sights. Strap in and let your legs dangle as you watch lifelike landscapes splash across a spherical screen. Drop into the **Port of Vancouver Discovery Centre** *(canadaplace.ca; free admission)*, on the ground floor of Canada Place, where hands-on displays and digital exhibits reveal how the country's busiest port operates behind the scenes.

### See Contemporary Indigenous Art  ART GALLERY
MAP: ❸ P34 **H2**

Opened in 2008, **Bill Reid Gallery of Northwest Coast Art** *(billreidgallery.ca; adult/youth $13/6)* is Canada's only public art gallery dedicated to the contemporary Indigenous art of the Northwest Coast. Hailed Haida artist Bill Reid (1920–98) was known for building bridges between Indigenous and settler people through his work as an artist, broadcaster and community activist. The gallery was named in his honor and showcases some of his artwork, as well as contemporary works by other Indigenous artists. Look for the full-scale totem pole carved by James Hart of Haida Gwaii, and the bronze masterpiece called *Mythic Messengers* by Reid himself.

### Enjoy a Show Under The Stars  THEATER
MAP: ❹ P34 **D1**

Stanley Park's charming **Malkin Bowl** provides an atmospheric alfresco stage for the city's summertime Theatre Under the Stars (TUTS) season, usually starring two interchanging Broadway musicals. It's hard to find a better place to catch a show, especially as the sun fades over the park's surrounding trees. Expect slick, professional and energetic productions.

### Visit Canada's Largest Aquarium  AQUARIUM
MAP: ❺ P34 **E1**

As Canada's largest aquarium and Stanley Park's biggest draw, the **Vancouver Aquarium** *(vanaqua.org; adult/child from $40/24)* is an obvious choice for connecting with coastal aquatic life. More than 65,000 animals can be found here. While it's a great place to get up-close with ocean life, the site is also a center for marine research, ocean literacy and climate activism. The fluffy sea otters have unofficial celebrity status in the city, and the sea lions (one weighs in at 1900lb) are a show-stopping sight. Other highlights include the **4D Experience**, a multi-sensory film that allows you to see, smell and feel the special effects; the educational **Wet Lab** space where kids learn about live invertebrates; and **Clownfish Cove**, an interactive play space.

### Shop Robson Street     SHOPPING
MAP: 6 P34 G6

For the best combination of renowned retail giants and small specialty shops, the **Robson Street** strip is Vancouver's most popular shopping spot. Spread along three city blocks (Burrard St to Jervis St), you will find 150 shops, lots of coffee shops and snack spots, and ample parking. Robson St is also a social gathering spot that brings crowds together for some of the city's liveliest events, including the 2010 Winter Olympics, Pride Parade and Canada Day celebrations. In summer, check out the Sunday Afternoon Salsa at Robson Square.

### Marvel at the Marine Building     ART DECO ARCHITECTURE
MAP: 7 P34 G4

Vancouver's most romantic old-school tower block and best art deco building is the elegant 22-story **Marine Building**, also a tribute to the city's maritime past. Check out its elaborate exterior of seahorses, lobsters and streamlined steamships, then nip into the lobby, which is like a walk-through artwork. Stained-glass panels and a polished floor inlaid with signs of the zodiac await, as well as two old-school phone booths – a nod back to the 1930s when the building was constructed.

---

 **DOWNTOWN EASTSIDE: A COMMUNITY IN NEED**

Downtown Eastside (DTES), primarily along East Hastings St at Main St, is home to a community in need. The area reflects Vancouver's deep-rooted socio-economic challenges, including poverty, addiction and mental health issues. Though it may seem unsettling, the DTES is also a place of resilience, with strong local support networks, harm-reduction programs and community organizations working to help those in need. Visitors are encouraged to approach with empathy, understanding and caution. Only explore the outer edges of Gastown or Chinatown on foot during daylight, stick to main roads like Powell St or Pender St, and avoid alleyways and quiet side streets, especially at night.

## LISTINGS

# Best Places for...

**$** Budget  **$$** Midrange  **$$$** Top End

**See p34** for map of locations

## Eating

### Affordable Eats

**Japadog $**
 **8** G6

A Japanese take on the traditional hot dog, this is an iconic Vancouver stop. Try the *kurobuta terimayo* (often simply called 'terimayo'), a Japadog fan favorite. *japadog.com; 10am-3am, to 4am Fri & Sat*

**Yasma $**
**9** D2

Syrian and Lebanese cuisine. You'll find modern takes on Middle Eastern staples, ranging from flavorful dips made from scratch (the muhammara dip is a must-try) to lamb dishes. *yasma.ca; 4-10pm Wed & Thu, to 10:30pm Fri & Sat*

**Meat & Bread $**
 **10** F5

Robson St location of Vancouver's best made-to-order hot sandwich mini-chain, serving regular faves like crispy porchetta, gooey grilled cheese and the ever-changing daily special. *meatandbread.com; 8am-8pm*

**Heritage Asian Eatery $**
**11** F4

Contemporary hole-in-the-wall favored by locals, this friendly fusion joint specializes in hearty rice bowls (duck or pork belly recommended) made with top-notch ingredients. *eatheritage.ca; 11:30am-8:30pm Mon-Fri, from noon Sat & Sun*

**Peaked Pies $**
 **12** C3

The Vancouver satellite of Whistler's popular Australian-themed pie shop, this comfort-food haven specializes in single-portion savory pie varieties including beef curry, steak and mushroom, and even ground kangaroo. *peakedpies.com; 9am-9pm Mon-Fri, from 8am Sat & Sun*

**Tacofino $$**
**13** F4

Fresh West Coast flavors meet Mexican food staples at this street-food-style spot. Pacific cod tacos and crunchy *carnitas* beckon taco-loving crowds, day and night. *tacofino.com; 8am-4pm Mon-Fri*

**Fanny Bay Oyster Bar & Shellfish Market $$**
**14** G6

Family-owned tide-to-table seafood spot. The SunSeeker oyster variety is superb, slightly sweet with a pleasing saline finish. *fannybayoysters.com; 2-10pm*

### Breakfast & Brunch

**Nero Belgian Waffle Bar $**
**15** F6

Try a cup of lavender London fog latte paired with a plate of authentic, freshly made Brussels or Liège waffles at this buzzing brunch spot on Seymour St. *nerowafflebar.com; 8am-10pm Sun-Thu, to 11pm Fri & Sat*

**Jam Cafe $**
 **16** H5

The city's best (and busiest) brunch spot, serving up homestyle options. The big breakfast bowls are best, opt for the Charlie Bowl or Later Tater Bowl (add pulled pork). *jamcafes.com; 8am-2:30pm, to 3pm Fri-Sat*

### Cafe Medina 💰💰
 G5

Finding a table can be tricky at this lively, wood-floored breakfast-brunch-lunch favorite. Light and fluffy waffles come with gourmet toppings, including raspberry-caramel and chocolate-lavender. *medinacafe.com; 8am-3pm Mon-Fri, from 9am Sat & Sun*

### Twisted Fork Bistro 💰💰
18 E6

Granville Strip's best brunch, this narrow art-lined bistro feels as if it should be somewhere else. Go the Benny eggs route, with pulled pork or smoked salmon (or both). *forkandfriends.ca; 9am-2pm*

### Fine Dining

### Teahouse in Stanley Park 💰💰
 A1

This lovely spot serves contemporary West Coast classics, such as roasted BC sablefish, along with jaw-dropping sunset patio views over Burrard Inlet. It's a good place for weekend brunch. *vanouverdine.com/teahouse; 10:30am-10pm Thu-Mon*

### Acquafarina 💰💰💰
20 G5

Michelin-recommended Italian dining in a classy space with large wood-burning pizza ovens, a copper bar and soaring ceilings. The pizzas and pasta are top-notch. *acquafarina.com; 11am-10pm Tue-Thu, to 11pm Fri & Sat*

### Hawksworth 💰💰💰
21 H3

Created by and named after one of Vancouver's top chefs, the menu here fuses contemporary West Coast with international influences in dishes such as miso-marinated sablefish. *hawksworthrestaurant.com; 11:30am-10pm Mon-Fri, from 3pm Sat-Sun*

### Boulevard Kitchen & Oyster Bar 💰💰💰
 F5

Award-winning chefs Alex Chen and Roger Ma are the masterminds behind the sophisticated seafood-forward menu. Start with a seafood tower, a feast for the eyes and the belly. *boulevardvancouver.com; 3-11pm*

### Botanist 💰💰💰
 G4

Michelin-recommended restaurant in Fairmont Pacific Rim, serving locally sourced Pacific Northwest fare. Cocktails are top-notch. Try the dry-aged striploin beef or steamed sablefish, and save room for dessert. *botanistrestaurant.com; hours vary*

### Chambar 💰💰💰
24 H6

This giant brick-lined cave is a centerpoint of Vancouver's dining scene, serving an ever-changing all-day menu of sophisticated dishes inspired by Belgian, North African, Persian and Mediterranean influences. *chambar.com; 5-10pm Sun-Wed, to 11pm Thu-Sat*

### Le Crocodile 💰💰💰
 E5

Renovated and reopened by renowned chef Rob Feenie in 2024, this excellent Parisian-style dining room offers French fine dining at its best. *lecrocodilerestaurant.com; 11:30am-2:30pm & 5-10pm Tue-Fri, 5-10pm Sat & Sun*

### Five Sails Restaurant $$$
 H4

Located in the Pan Pacific Hotel, Five Sails is a city classic, with a recently reinvented menu in 2025 by new Chef Alex Kim, a Canadian culinary champion lauded for his elevated West Coast cuisine. *facebook.com/fivesails; 5-10pm*

# Drinking

## Cocktail Bars

### Botanist
see  G4

Vancouver's top cocktail bar. With head bartender Jeff Savage at the helm, Botanist combines chemist-like cocktail designs with amazing artistry to create magic in a glass. *botanistrestaurant.com; hours vary*

### Lift Bar & Grill
 E2

On warmer days, grab bevvies on this bustling rooftop bar and take in scenic Stanley Park views. In the mood for a cocktail? Try a rosemary fizz. *liftbarandgrill.com; 11:30am-10pm Mon-Fri, from 11am Sat & Sun*

### Uva Wine & Cocktail Bar
 F6

This European-inspired cafe-bar serves refined wines, creative cocktails and imported beers. Food is part of the mix (including shareable small plates) and there's a 2pm to 5pm happy hour. *uvavancouver.com; 7am-11pm Sun-Thu, to midnight Fri & Sat*

## Casual Pubs

### Fountainhead Pub
 E6

The area's loudest and proudest gay neighborhood pub, in Davie Village. This friendly joint is all about the patio, pints, pool and people-watching. *fthdpub.com; 11am-midnight Sun-Thu, to 1am Fri & Sat*

### Pumpjack Pub
 D5

A Davie Street staple serving the LGBTIQ+ community for more than 20 years. DJs, cocktails, craft beer, food trucks and a sunny patio make it a summer hot spot. *pumpjackpub.com; 1pm-3am*

### Stanley's Bar & Grill
31 D1

Tucked into one end of the century-old Stanley Park Pavilion. Snag a patio seat under red parasols and grab a beery respite after a day of park exploring. *stanleysbargrill.com; 11am-7pm*

## Coffee & Tea

### Caffè Artigiano
 G3

An international award winner for its barista skills and latte art, Artigiano has the locals frothing at the mouth with its rich java beverages. *caffeartigiano.com; 7am-5pm Mon-Fri, from 8am Sat & Sun*

### Delany's Coffee House
 C4

This laid-back, wood-and-art-lined neighborhood coffee bar is the Java-hugging heart of the West End's LGBTIQ+ community. Delany's is a good perch from which to catch the annual Pride Parade (if you can snag a seat). *delanyscoffee.com; 6am-6pm Mon-Fri, from 6:30am Sat & Sun*

### Caffè Mira
34 E6

Pop by this quaint plant-filled cafe for a coffee, matcha or unique latte (try a purple ube latte!). The pastries and sandwiches are equally delicious. *caffemira.com;*

*7:30am-5pm Mon-Fri, from 8:30am Sat & Sun*

# Shopping

## Specialty Shops

### Paper Hound
**35** H5

Proving the printed word is still loved, this small secondhand bookstore is a local favorite. A perfect spot for browsing, it tempts with tomes (mostly used, some new) on everything from nature and poetry to chaos theory. *paperhound.ca; 10am-6pm*

### Little Sister's Book & Art Emporium
**36** D5

Launched almost 40 years ago as one of the only LGBTIQ+ bookshops in Canada, Little Sister's is a bazaar of queer-positive tomes, plus magazines, clothing and toys of the adult type. *littlesisters.ca; 10am-10pm*

### Golden Age Collectables
**37** F5

One of Vancouver's oldest, best-known comic shops, Golden Age stocks old and new comic books, graphic novels, toys, manga, sports cards and more. *gacvan.com; noon-5pm*

### Mink Chocolates
**38** G4

The flagship location of this Vancouver-based artisan company, Mink crafts small-batch, hand-moulded bars and bonbons. Its cafe serves chocolate drinks, fondue and other treats. *minkchocolates.com; 7:30am-7pm Mon-Fri, from 9am Sat & Sun*

### Macleod's Books
**39** H5

From its creaky floorboards to scuzzy carpets and teetering piles of books, this legendary locals' fave is a great place to peruse a cornucopia of used tomes. Browse all subjects, from dance to the occult. *instagram.com/macleodsbooks;11am-5:30pm*

### Vancouver Pen Shop
**40** H5

Pleasingly old-fashioned, where friendly staff greet you and the items sold are a nod to a bygone age when fine pens and penmanship were prized. Writing tools for every budget, plus cool stationery and retro Vancouver prints. *facebook.com/vanpenshop; 10am-6pm Mon-Sat*

## Art & Music

### Vancouver Art Gallery Store
**41** G3

Pick up art books, posters, unique gifts and Canadian-made items, including a wide selection of Emily Carr merchandise. Partial proceeds go towards the VAG's exhibitions, education initiatives and public programs. *shop.vanartgallery.bc.ca; 10am-5:30pm*

### Bill Reid Gallery Shop
**42** H2

Shop for traditional and contemporary Indigenous artwork and accessories, including hand-painted sculptures, finely crafted jewelry, framed and unframed prints and more. *billreidgallery.ca; 10am-5pm*

### Beat Street Records
**43** H5

Independently owned and community-based, this store is made for music lovers, musicians, DJs, artists and collectors. It has over 50,000 records in the store, and more in its warehouse. *beatstreet.ca; hours vary*

## ⭐ TOP EXPERIENCE

# West Coast Whale Watching

Vancouver's coast is home to incredible marine life, and there's no shortage of tours to take you out for a look. Orcas (killer whales), humpbacks and gray whales, along with seals, sea lions, porpoises and seabirds are just some of the aquatic animals you can encounter.

**PLANNING TIP**
May to November is peak whale-watching season, but whales can be spotted year-round. Many tours depart directly from the docks on Granville Island.

### Sea Views

Choose your boat (12-person zodiac to cutting-edge catamaran) and hit the seas. Ninety-minute waterfront rides to half-day whale-watching tours with **Prince of Whales** *(princeofwhales.com; tours from $85)* depart from Granville Island and other city locations. Expect stunning views and wondrous wildlife sightings.

### Observe Orcas

Vancouver's coastal waters are part of the Salish Sea ecosystem and among the world's top spots for orca sightings (pictured). Bigg's (transient) orcas, known for hunting marine mammals like seals and porpoises, are the most common. Resident orcas are fish eaters that mainly rely on Chinook salmon: southern residents are critically endangered and seen less frequently around Vancouver today; northern residents are more often found further up the coast. Tours are led by certified guides who follow strict wildlife-friendly practices. Many operators belong to the Pacific Whale Watch Association.

Scan this QR code to book a tour with Prince of Whales tours.

### Watch for Whales

Humpback whales are most commonly seen on whale-watching tours. They migrate to BC's coastal

IACOMINO FRIMAGES/SHUTTERSTOCK

waters to feed on krill and small fish, primarily in summer. Less common gray whales can also be spotted during their migration between Mexico and Alaska, particularly in the spring, although they're less common in the Vancouver area itself. Minke whales are occasionally seen, but are more elusive than baleen whales and harder to spot due to their quick surfacing behavior.

## Beyond Whales

Whales may be the main draw, but Vancouver's nutrient-rich coastal waters are home to a wide range of other marine life. Spot playful porpoises, curious harbor seals, barking sea lions, soaring bald eagles and, if you're lucky, a sea otter swimming by. Jellyfish, including moon jellies and lion's mane jellies, are frequent visitors.

**QUICK BREAK**
Perch on the patio of Tap & Barrel Bridges for a bevy and snack with views of Burrard St Bridge, floating mini ferries and boats bobbing in the harbor.

# Explore
# Gastown & Chinatown

As the city's oldest downtown neighborhood and a designated national historic site, Gastown combines cobblestone streets and late 19th- and early 20th-century architecture with modern art galleries, chic shops and trendy bars. The charming 12-block district, best explored on foot, is a vibrant hub for shopping, dining and entertainment. Just next door lies one of Canada's largest and most culturally-rich Chinatown districts – a lively community filled with authentic dim sum restaurants, traditional bakeries, specialty food shops and tucked-away cocktail lounges. Both neighborhoods offer plenty of hidden spots, historical landmarks and photo-worthy places showcasing the city's diverse culture and fascinating past.

## Getting Around

 **Train**
You'll find SkyTrain's Waterfront Station in the west of Gastown. The Stadium-Chinatown Station is at the edge of Chinatown, south of Gastown.

 **Bus**
Bus 14 heads northwards from downtown's Granville St, then along Hastings, handy for access to both Gastown and Chinatown. Bus 10 connects the two neighborhoods. Buses 3, 4, 7 and 8 also service the area.

 **Car**
There's paid metered parking and patrolled parking lots scattered throughout Gastown and Chinatown.

### THE BEST

**CITY GARDEN** Dr. Sun Yat-Sen Classical Chinese Garden (p56)

**ASIAN CUISINE** Phnom Penh (p64)

**PHOTO SPOT** Gastown Steam Clock (p55)

**SHOPPING STREET** Historic Gastown (p62)

**CULTURE MUSEUM** Chinese-Canadian Museum (p62)

Historic Gastown (p62)
MO WU/SHUTTERSTOCK

# GASTOWN & CHINATOWN

## EXPLORE

Map locations:

- Gastown Steam Clock (A1)
- Dominion Building (A2)
- Flack Block (A2)
- Powell Street (Paueru-gai) (B2)
- Gaoler's Mews (B1)
- Hotel Europe (C1)
- Chinese-Canadian Museum (C3)
- Koot Thing Vintage (C3)
- Dr Sun Yat-Sen Classical Chinese Garden (D4)
- Vancouver Police Museum & Archives (E2)
- Firehall Arts Centre (E2)
- Rickshaw Theatre (E3)
- Chinatown Storytelling Centre (E3)
- Chinatown BBQ (D3)
- Hogan's Alley (E4)
- Oppenheimer Park (F2)

Streets and areas shown: Railway St, Alexander St, Powell St, E Cordova St, E Hastings St, E Pender St, Keefer St, E Georgia St, Gore Ave, Dunlevy Ave, Jackson Ave, Main St, Columbia St, Carrall St, Abbott St, Cambie St, Hamilton St, Water St, Cordova St, W Hastings St, W Pender St, Keefer Pl, Waterfront Rd, Blood Alley, Trounce Al.

Landmarks: Portside Park, Andy Livingstone Park, Victory Sq, GASTOWN, CHINATOWN, Stadium-Chinatown SkyTrain.

### For more see

- Top Experiences ★ p55
- Experiences ✦ p60
- Eating ✕ p64
- Drinking 🍸 p66
- Shopping 🛍 p67

0.1 miles / 200 m

54

⭐ **TOP EXPERIENCE**

# Gastown Steam Clock

On Vancouver's oldest street in Gastown, the **Steam Clock** is one of only a few still operating and is among the city's popular photo spots. Its fame has earned it spots on Nickelback's *Here and Now* (2011) album cover, and in the 2023 film *The Hitman*.

### Historical Timepiece

The Gastown Steam Clock was built by self-taught Canadian clockmaker Raymond Saunders in 1977. The clock was originally powered by steam from the city's underground heating system. Although it now runs on electricity for better accuracy, the clock still emits steam from its top every hour.

### Westminster Whistles

Along with the steam show, the clock toots a series of steam-driven whistles. Four times an hour, it performs a version of London's 'Westminster Chimes' using five finely tuned brass pipes. At the top of each hour, a longer whistle blows – the tune originally from a Canadian Pacific Railway steam vessel.

### Shifting Gears

Inside the clock, there's a fascinating mix of old-world mechanics and modern engineering. The clock uses steam from Vancouver's central heating system to power a small steam engine driving the clock's mechanical display. The timekeeping is regulated by an electric mechanism. On the quarter hour, steam is released through a series of valves to play the 'Westminster Chimes' on five steam whistles.

MAP P54 **A1**

**PLANNING TIP**
Visit just before the quarter-hour. The clock whistles and releases steam every 15 minutes, with a longer display on the hour. Arrive a few minutes early for the best viewing spot.

Scan this QR code for an eerie guided history tour of Gastown.

## ⭐ TOP EXPERIENCE

# Dr Sun Yat-Sen Classical Chinese Garden

Opened for Vancouver's Expo '86, this delightful oasis was the first Chinese 'scholars' garden' to be built outside Asia, and is one of the city's most-beloved ornamental green spaces. Wrapped with tile-topped walls and centered on a mirror-calm pond fringed by twisting trees, its covered walkways offer a tranquil respite from clamorous Chinatown.

MAP P54 **C4**

**PLANNING TIP**
Arrive closer to opening in summer to experience the tranquility before the crowds roll in. Guided tours run hourly during the summer, and several times a day the rest of the year. Check the schedule online.

Scan this QR code for tickets, events and workshops.

### Harmonious Design

With symbol-heavy architecture that feels centuries old – walled courtyards, small bridges, flared-roof buildings and patterned sidewalks fashioned from pebble mosaics – the **garden** *(vancouverchinesegarden.com; adult/child $16/12)* is highly photogenic. Large limestone rocks that look as though they were imported from the moon give the garden a mystical, almost otherworldly feel; they were actually hauled from Lake Tai in China. Admission includes an optional 45-minute guided tour in which you can learn about its Taoist principles of balance and harmony, and the symbolism behind the placement of the gnarled pine trees, winding covered pathways and ancient limestone formations.

### Natural Highlights

The garden's large, lily pad–covered pond is as calm as a sheet of green glass – except when its resident neon-orange koi carp break the surface in hopes of snagging food from passersby (don't feed them). These are not the only critters to call this watery haven home. Look closely at rocks poking out the water to spot turtles dozing in the sun. Ducks, frogs and beady-eyed herons are also frequent visitors. Plant-wise, spot pine, bamboo, flowering plum trees and pots of decades-old bonsai.

RIEKEPHOTOS/SHUTTERSTOCK

The adjacent **Dr Sun Yat-Sen Park** isn't quite as elaborate as its classical sister, but it's free to enter and is a pleasant oasis with its whispering grasses, fishpond and pagoda.

## Traditional Tea

Before leaving the Dr Sun Yat-Sen Classical Chinese Garden, enjoy a complimentary cup of traditional Chinese tea. If you're visiting on a Saturday or Sunday, join a public tea ceremony. The sessions offer a special opportunity to experience a tradition that's been part of Chinese culture for thousands of years. During the ceremony, taste two different kinds of tea and explore how they differ in aroma, flavor and character.

**QUICK BREAK**
Tuck into a retro-style booth and lunch on family-style barbecue dishes at **Chinatown BBQ**.

# Walk Chinatown

One of North America's largest, most historic Chinatown districts, Chinatown is ripe for exploring on foot. Admire tile-topped heritage buildings, traditional grocery and apothecary stores, and street lamps adorned with golden dragons. Allow time for the 'hood's amazing restaurants and cocktail bars.

| START | END | LENGTH |
|---|---|---|
| Chinatown Millennium Gate | Vancouver Police Museum | 1.5km; one hour |

### 1 Ornamental Gate
Built in 2002, **Chinatown Millennium Gate** is a striking landmark featuring three traditional Chinese arches topped with terracotta-tiled roofs and an elaborately painted upper section. Inscribed with the message 'Remember the past and look forward to the future,' the gate symbolizes a bridge between East and West, honoring the vital contributions of Chinese-Canadians.

### 2 Garden Escape
Enjoy a respite from Chinatown's clamorous streets at **Dr Sun Yat-Sen Classical Chinese Garden** (p56), a peaceful site with cobbled pathways. Watch for carp and turtles in the mirror-calm pond, and end with a complimentary cup of traditional tea.

### 3 Rail Workers Memorial
Wander across the small paved plaza near the garden's entrance to find an intriguing **bronze memorial** set in bright-red wall tiles. It recalls the contribution of Chinese workers to the enormous project of building Canada's railway system in the 1880s.

### 4 The 'Other' Gate
A few steps away is a ghostly white **alternative Chinatown gate**. Smaller than the original Chinese Millennium Gate, it was built for Vancouver's Expo '86 and moved here after the event.

### 5 Lunch Break
Pop into **Chinatown BBQ** for lunch or an early dinner. The retro-chic Cantonese barbecue shop serves simple, perfectly prepared platters of meat and rice. The must-try is the 'four treasures plate' – a hearty combo of roast pork, BBQ pork, soy chicken and salted egg over rice.

### 6 History Stop
A showcase of Vancouver's Chinese Canadian history, **Chinatown Storytelling Centre** includes a life-size diorama, an interactive etiquette table and a living legacy project highlighting the most famous Chinese Canadians from past and present.

### 7 Keefer Street Stores
Chinatown is lined with a fascinating fusion of old-fashioned and far newer **storefronts**. Exploring Keefer St, you'll find traditional grocery shops next to hipster coffeehouses and quirky gift shops.

### 8 Through a Blue Lens
The city's crime-ridden past is on colorful display at the under-the-radar **Vancouver Police Museum & Archives** (p61). This is North America's oldest police museum, housed in a heritage building on the outskirts of Chinatown. Don't miss its historic crime exhibits and preserved mortuary room.

## EXPERIENCES

### Discover Chinese-Canadian History  CULTURE
MAP: ① P54 D3

The **Chinatown Storytelling Centre** *(chinatownstorytellingcentre.org; adult/child $12.50/free)* showcases Vancouver's Chinese-Canadian history. Find a life-sized diorama of the first housing units built for workers who arrived from China to work on the Canadian Pacific Railway in the 1880s. You'll also find an interactive etiquette table and the Robert HN Ho Living Legacy Project, which highlights the personal stories of Vancouver's most prominent Chinese-Canadians from the 1880s to the present day. This is Canada's first permanent exhibit dedicated to the Chinese-Canadian journey, and the individual stories shared create a truly unique perspective on the Asian community in Vancouver. Stroll through solo, or book a guided tour (only available for groups of 10 or more).

### Take In a Local Performance  THEATER

Catch a show at one of the area's standout venues. Housed in a historic former fire station, **Firehall Arts Centre** (MAP: ② P54 E2; *firehallartscentre.ca; tickets from $30*) is a leading player on Vancouver's independent theater scene, presenting culturally diverse contemporary drama and dance, often with an emphasis on emerging talent. It features a lively licensed lounge on site and is a key venue during July's **Dancing on the Edge** *(dancingontheedge.org)*. For live music, head to the revamped **Rickshaw Theatre** (MAP: ③ P54 E3; *liveatrickshaw.com; tickets from $15),* once a grungy 1970s cinema, but now a funky stage for punk and indie acts. The venue has a huge mosh area near the stage, and rows of theater-style seats at the back.

---

**FOODIE FAVORITES**

*Recommended by Leila Kwok, food photographer. @leilalikes*

First, indulge in a fusion of flavors and culture at **Torafuku** (MAP: ④ P54 D4), where East meets West in exquisite dishes and cocktails crafted with precision and creativity. Next, step into Phnom Penh (p64), an authentic Cambodian spot, and savor the rich aromas and bold spices that bring its traditional recipes to life. It offers an unforgettable taste of Southeast Asia, from noodles to its famous butter beef. Finally, visit steakhouse star Elisa (p82), where prime cuts are expertly prepared and grilled to perfection. Savor the exceptional flavors that will satisfy even the most discerning palates.

## Pop By the Powell Street Festival FESTIVAL

While many early immigrants to Vancouver came from China, others settled here from across Asia. Just east of Chinatown, Japanese Canadians (Nikkei) established a vibrant community known as **Paueru-gai** (MAP: **5** P54 **B2**) or Powell Street (sometimes called Japantown). It was once home to residences, shops and businesses serving the city's early Japanese population. Centered in an area around **Oppenheimer Park** (MAP: **6** P54 **F2**), the intriguing historic district is worth a wander. Some of the city's oldest small wooden homes here are a reminder of the sometimes-forgotten past.

The best time to visit is early August when the weekend-long **Powell Street Festival** *(powellstreetfestival.com)* celebrates Japanese heritage and culture. One of Canada's largest and longest-running community arts festivals, the event includes traditional music, vibrant performances, inviting food stands and a mini-market with stalls selling authentic arts and crafts. The festival's Omikoshi shrine procession is a standout – the loud, energetic and interactive community celebration sees a symbolic Shinto deity carried through the streets in a portable shrine.

## See The City's Past Through a Blue Lens MUSEUM
MAP: **7** P54 **E2**

Criminal cases, unsolved murder mysteries and forensic science are just some of the things you can discover at the **Vancouver Police Museum & Archives** *(vancouverpolicemuseum.ca; adult/child $13.50/10)*. Housed in an authentic heritage building, the museum was first opened in 1986 by the Police Historical Society to celebrate the centennial anniversary of the city's police department. Featured exhibits include **True Crime**, a deep-dive into the city's most chilling criminal cases, highlighting real cases and evidence. **Behind the Lines: A Traffic Story** is a behind-the-lens look at the history of Vancouver's evolving traffic scene, from carriages to riot control and present-day road safety. In the **Morgue and Autopsy Suite**, you get to peek into the morgue and autopsy suite where pathologists and coroners worked to uncover the city's most notable true crimes from 1932 until 1980.

## Uncover Vancouver's Hidden Black History CULTURE
MAP: **8** P54 **E4**

Discover Vancouver's rich yet often overlooked Black history on a 'Live the City's Black history' walking tour with **Hogan's Alley Tours** *(planher.ca/hogans-alley-tours; $40)*. Led by a local historian and teacher, the tour takes you through the Strathcona neighborhood. It passes through Hogan's Alley, once the heart of Vancouver's Black community before displacement by the viaduct construction in the 1970s. Stops along the alley include a larger-than-life Jimi Hendrix portrait honoring the musician's Vancouver roots, and the locations of past churches, cafes and meeting spaces that served as cultural hubs from the 1850s. The tour reflects on the erasure of a neighborhood and concludes with a hopeful vision for restoration and activism, highlighting the Hogan's Alley Society's ongoing efforts to preserve this vital part of Vancouver's history. It offers an intimate glimpse into how Vancouver's Black community shaped the city's cultural history and the groups advocating for its recognition today.

### Stroll Historic Gastown ARCHITECTURE

Vancouver's oldest downtown neighborhood combines antique lampposts and heritage brick buildings with modern art galleries, fashion boutiques, souvenir shops and trendy bars. In 2009 Gastown was named a national historic site for its intact Victorian architecture and significance as modern Vancouver's first neighborhood.

Tourists gather in Gastown today for the photo ops alone. But the historic 12-block stretch is also a buzzing hub for shopping and entertainment, best enjoyed on foot. In summer, check out the pop-up live music series, **Gastown Thursday Nights** *(gastown.org/thursdaynights; 4-7pm Thu)*, which brings live music to various locations around Gastown. For brunch, book a table at **Water St Cafe** (p65) in a 1906 heritage building; the restaurant has been a Vancouver landmark since 1988.

### Shop for Vintage Finds SHOPPING
MAP: 9 P54 C3

Gastown and Chinatown are not only known for their cool, eclectic shops. In recent years, they have become hotspots for vintage shopping. Tucked away on side streets, particularly Columbia St between E Pender St and E Hastings St, you'll find a growing collection of curated vintage stores like **Kool Thing Vintage** *(koolthingvintage.com)*, offering everything from retro fashion to unique homewares. Alongside secondhand treasures, find shops focused on fair trade, organic goods, small-batch and slow fashion, local plant stores, and B-Corp businesses – all part of Vancouver's thriving, ethically conscious shopping scene.

### Explore the Chinese-Canadian Museum MUSEUM
MAP: 10 P54 C3

Dedicated to celebrating the Chinese-Canadian community and their contributions to the history and heritage of Vancouver, the **Chinese-Canadian Museum** *(chinesecanadianmuseum.ca; adult/child $15/10)* opened in 2023 in the oldest brick structure found in the area. The heritage

## VANCOUVER'S OLDEST STREET

Just weeks after adopting the name 'Vancouver' in 1886, the city was nearly erased by the Great Fire. Instead of fleeing, locals rebuilt the area, this time in brick and stone. The heart of this rebirth was **Maple Tree Square**, where citizens first gathered to lay out plans for a new city. From here, the short thoroughfare of Carrall Street branched out from the square to link the historic center of Gastown to Chinatown, and beyond. Though the Carrall area later fell into decline, heritage advocates and gentrification helped clean it up. Restored storefronts and taverns in Carrall today stand as proud reminders of the city's past.

---

building dates to 1889. Inside, you'll find period rooms and permanent exhibits like 'A Soldier for All Seasons,' highlighting the Chinese-Canadian experiences on the front lines. You'll also find contemporary art displays and immersive exhibits where travel, pop culture, migration and music history collide.

### Mingle with Artists & Street Performers    FESTIVAL

During November's **Eastside Culture Crawl** – a four-day festival featuring the works of 500+ artists – local artists open their studios, houses and workshops to art-loving visitors who wander from site to site. Festival locations stretch eastwards from the north end of Main St, and you can spend your time walking the streets looking for the next hot spot, which is typically just around the corner. Look out for the occasional street performer keeping things lively and be sure to incorporate a coffee-shop pit stop along the way. The event is a great opportunity to buy one-of-a-kind artwork souvenirs for that hard-to-buy-for person back home (you know the one).

### Photo Ops Beyond the Steam Clock    ARCHITECTURE

Walking along Water St, you'll likely bump into a gaggle of visitors snapping photos of the **Steam Clock** (p55), a freestanding timepiece famous for its time-marking steam-whistle displays. But Gastown is full of additional photo opportunities providing you know where to go. Scan for cool architectural details at the **Dominion Building** (MAP: 11 P54 **A2**) and the **Flack Block** (MAP: 12 P54 **A2**); gawk at **Gaoler's Mews** (MAP: 13 P54 **C2**) with its heritage red-brick and cobblestone courtyard, and be sure to snap a shot of the wedge-shaped **Hotel Europe** (MAP: 14 P54 **C2**; or Flatiron Building), a landmark in the city since it was built in 1909.

# LISTINGS

See p54 for map of locations

# Best Places for...

$ Budget   $$ Midrange   $$$ Top End

## Eating

### Snacks & Sandwiches

**Meat & Bread** $

🟢15  A2

Arrive early to sidestep the lunchtime line-ups at Vancouver's favorite sandwich mini-chain. Snag a spot at the shared long table, and try the daily-changing special or the ever-popular, juicy porchetta sandwich. The finger-licking grilled cheese is also delicious. *meatandbread.com; 11am-4pm Sun-Wed, to 8pm Thu-Sat*

**Say Hey Cafe** $

🟢16  D3

This hole-in-the-wall eatery fuses a friendly hipster vibe with a menu of seriously satisfying submarine sandwiches. The selection, on toasted sesame-studded buns, ranges from meatball and all-day breakfast hoagies to a juicily delicious mortadella-packed option. *sayheycafe.ca; 8am-4pm Mon-Fri*

**Hunnybee Bruncheonette** $

🟢17  E4

A bright cafe overlooking Strathcona's painted heritage houses (snag an outdoor row seat on sunny days), the elevated comfort food here ranges from breakfast buns stuffed with shiitake-scrambled eggs to made-from-scratch hot sandwiches. *hunnybee.ca; 8am-4pm*

### Noodles & Pho

**Fat Mao** $

🟢18  E4

Best known for serving hand-pulled noodles and tasty Thai-style noodle soups made with flavorful broths. Fat Mao is one of the top restaurants backed by Chef Angus An (also Maenam and Popina Cantina). *fatmaonoodles.com; hours vary*

**Ramen Butcher** $

🟢19  E4

The signature thin noodles here come in several broth-bowl varieties, with slabs of slow-cooked pork; the garlicky red spicy ramen is a must-try. Still have some soup in your bowl? They'll toss in a second serving of noodles for free. *theramenbutcher.com; noon-9:30pm Wed-Sun, to 10pm Fri & Sat*

**DD Mau** $

🟢20  D3

Found below Fortune Sound Club, family-owned DD Mau serves authentic Vietnamese cuisine with a twist. Favorites include pho, banh mi, lemongrass chicken and pork belly baos – flavorful, fresh and satisfying. *ddmau.ca; hours vary*

### Global Cuisine

**Phnom Penh** $

🟢21  E4

The dishes at this bustling local legend are split between Cambodian and Vietnamese soul-food classics. It's the highly addictive chicken wings and their lovely pepper sauce that keep regulars loyal. *instagram.com/phnompenh.restaurant; 11am-9pm Wed-Mon*

### Tacofino Taco Bar $
 C2

This food-truck favorite stars a huge dining room featuring stylish geometric-patterned floors, hive-like lampshades and a tiny back patio. The simple menu focuses on a handful of taco options, plus nachos, soups and tequila flights. *tacofino.com; 11am-10pm*

### Nuba $$
23 A2

Tucked under the landmark Dominion Building, this Lebanese restaurant serves tasty, surprisingly filling mezze dishes, including excellent hummus and falafel. Dive straight into a shareable 'la feast' for two covering all bases. *nuba.ca; 11:30am-9pm Sun-Thu, to 10pm Fri & Sat*

## Upscale Dining
### Bao Bei $$
24 D4

This Chinese brasserie is a seductive dinner destination. Bringing a contemporary edge to Asian cuisine are tapas-sized, MSG-free dishes such as *shao bing* (stuffed Chinese flatbread), delectable dumplings and spicy-chicken steamed buns. *bao-bei.ca; 5:30-10pm Sun-Thu, to midnight Fri & Sat*

### St Lawrence Restaurant $$$
25 E2

This Michelin-starred spot serves succulent French-Canadian cuisine in a wood-floored bistro that transports you to Montreal. Seasonal dishes are made with local ingredients. If it's on the menu, the trout in brown-butter sauce is a must. *stlawrencerestaurant.com; 5-10:30pm Tue-Sun*

### Kissa Tanto $$$
26 E3

Tucked into the upper story of a delightfully faded building in Chinatown, Kissa Tanto offers a fusion of Italian and Japanese cuisine. Notable dishes include the fried whole fish and the lasagna made with Japanese ingredients like miso. *kissatanto.com; hours vary Wed-Sun*

### L'Abattoir $$$
27 C2

Gastown's best special-occasion restaurant, this candlelit, brick-lined spot makes an art of attending to every detail. Be careful not to fill up on starters of seared scallops and baked oysters before tucking into their French-influenced West Coast mains. *labattoir.ca; 5-11pm Tue-Sun*

### Water St Cafe $$$
 A1

Gastown's prime patio (you can see the Steam Clock from your seat), serving Italian cuisine with West Coast influences, and a solid wine list. After dinner, head upstairs to 2nd Floor Gastown, its live music venue, for a nightcap. *waterstreetcafe.ca; 11am-10pm Mon-Fri, from 10am Sat & Sun*

## Vegetarian & Vegan
### MeeT in Gastown $
29 C2

Busy at times, but worth the wait for a wide-ranging array of herbivore- and carnivore-pleasing choices, from rice bowls and mac 'n' cheese (made from vegan cashew 'cheese') to hearty burgers and poutine-like fries. *eatmeet.ca; hours vary Wed-Sun*

### Birds & the Beets $
30 C2

A friendly, local-favorite hangout with a small menu of delicious, made-to-order salads, sandwiches and breakfast items. Try the avocado-and-poached-egg brioche sandwich. *birdsandbeets.ca; 8am-4pm*

### Virtuous Pie
**31** D4

The pizzas are entirely plant-based at this inviting little vegan pizzeria. With its communal tables, exposed brick and mood lighting, expect cool lounge bar vibes. Arrive off-peak and pick from a menu of one-person pies. *virtuouspie.com; hours vary*

# Drinking

## Cocktail Bars
### Laowai
**32** E4

A hidden speakeasy tucked behind the freezer door of dumpling stall BLND TGER (ask for the #7 to get access). Laowai's decor nods to 1930s Shanghai. Chinese-inspired cocktails like bai tai – a unique twist on the classic mai tai – are lauded here. *laowai.ca; hours vary*

### Keefer Bar

This dark, narrow and atmospheric bar has been claimed by local cocktail-loving coolsters since day one. Drop in for anything from perfectly prepared rosemary gimlets to an excellent whiskey menu and tasty tapas. The steam buns are top notch). *thekeeferbar.com; 4pm-1am Sun-Thu, to 2am Fri & Sat*

## Casual Pubs
### Alibi Room
 D1

Vancouver's best craft-beer tavern pours a near-legendary roster of 50-plus drafts, many from celebrated BC breweries including Four Winds, Yellow Dog and Dageraad Brewing. *alibi.ca; 4-10pm Mon-Thu, to midnight Fri-Sun*

### Guilt & Co
**35** C2

This cavelike bar beneath Gastown's sidewalks is a brilliant venue for live music. Most shows are pay-what-you-can and range from trumpet jazz to performances by singer-songwriters. There's a great cocktail list, and a small menu of draft beers. *guiltandcompany.com; 6pm-midnight Mon-Wed, to 1am Thu, to 2am Fri & Sat*

### Six Acres
 C2

Gastown's coziest tavern, with a carefully chosen draft- and bottled-beer list. There's a small, animated summer patio out front, but inside (especially upstairs) is great for hiding in a chatty, candlelit corner. *sixacres.ca; hours vary*

### Steamworks Brew Pub
 A1

This huge brewpub at the edge of Gastown serves several house-made beers, including crisp pilsners, hoppy IPAs and seasonal small-batch beers. The best of the bunch is the malty pale ale, ideal for slow afternoons at an alfresco table. *steamworks.com; 11:30am-midnight Mon-Fri, from 11am Sat & Sun*

## Coffee & Tea
### Revolver
 A2

Gastown's coolest see-and-be-seen coffee shop, serving expertly prepared, top-quality java. Aim for a little booth table or, if they're taken (they usually are), hit the large communal table next door. *revolvercoffee.ca; 7:30am-5pm Mon-Sat*

### Nemesis Coffee
 A2

Hip, light-filled coffeehouse lauded for its artisanal pastries and all-day brunch, plus coffee, tea and kombucha. Pick a pour-over paired with duck and waffles. *nemesis.coffee; 8am-4pm*

### Timbertrain Coffee
**40** A1

On the edge of Gastown, this little coffee shop is filled with quirky details (look for the Rolodex of cafe-goers' loyalty cards). Pick a slow pour-over, and perch on a bench or in a hidden nook. *timbertrain.ca; 8am-4pm Mon-Fri, 9am-5pm Sat & Sun*

# Shopping

## Vintage Shops
### Gore St Vintage
**41** E4

Traipse through this two-level warehouse-like shop to find a top-tier selection of vintage tees, retro frocks and stonewashed denim, as well as vendors selling the latest vintage trends and styles. *noon-8pm*

### Community Thrift & Vintage Frock Shoppe
**42** C2

This nonprofit social enterprise sells a cornucopia of vintage women's clothing, from 1970s print dresses to elegant silk tops and printed T-shirts of old bands you may have never heard of. *communitythriftandvintage.com; 11am-7pm Mon-Sat, noon-5pm Sun*

## Shoes & Accessories
### John Fluevog Shoes
**43** C1

Like an art gallery for shoes, this alluringly cavernous store showcases the famed footwear of local designer Fluevog, whose men's and women's boots and brogues are what Doc Martens would have become if they'd stayed interesting and cutting-edge. *fluevog.com; 10am-6pm*

### Herschel Supply Co
**44** A1

The friendly flagship store of this hot Vancouver-based bags-and-accessories brand is a must-see for Herschel fans. Inside a beautifully restored, artwork-lined Gastown heritage building, you'll find a huge array of the company's signature daypacks. *herschel.com; 10am-6pm Sun-Mon, to 7pm Fri & Sat*

### Shayelily Jewelry
**45** C1

Make your own charm bracelet or jewelry keepsake in a chic second-floor space: there a huge selection of options, including fresh-water pearls and glass-blown or ceramic beads. The Italian charm bracelets are popular. *shayelilyjewelry.com; hours vary*

## Books & Music
### Massy Books
**46** E4

This delightful Chinatown bookstore is lined with tall stacks of well-curated, mostly used titles. There's an impressively large selection of Indigenous-themed books, alongside good selections covering travel, history and literature. *massybooks.com; hours vary Thu-Tue*

### Vinyl Records
**47** A2

Rifle through a huge array of albums at this vinyl-lover's dream. Make sure you strike up a conversation with the owner – he knows exactly where everything is. *11am-6pm Mon-Sat, from noon Sun*

# Explore
# Yaletown & Granville Island

These coastal communities straddle tranquil False Creek. Yaletown, a revitalized warehouse district, is now one of the city's most chic areas where cool boutiques and posh urban patios draw crowds. Yaletown's waterfront parks, including expansive green spaces David Lam Park and George Wainborn Park, are connected by a seawall and inspire grassy picnics with water views. A short ride on a mini pedestrian ferry takes you to Granville Island, combining industrial heritage with modern architecture. Lauded as Vancouver's artisan capital, it's home to western Canada's biggest public market. Remnants from the area's factory past can still be spotted throughout.

## Getting Around

 **Bus**
Parking can be tricky in peak season, June to August, so consider arriving by bus. Several lines serve the area – an easy alternative to driving.

 **Bike**
Cycling is the best way to explore Granville Island and Yaletown. Some mini ferries carry bikes, allowing for flexibility.

 **Ferry**
Aquabus runs from Hornby St to Yaletown; False Creek Ferry connects Kitsilano to Science World. Both stop at Granville Island Public Market.

## THE BEST

**KIDS SHOP**
Kids Market (p78)

**MARKET** Granville Island Public Market (p72)

**THEATER VENUE** Granville Island Stage (p80)

**SPORTS STADIUM** BC Place Stadium (p78)

**ARTS & CRAFTS** Railspur Alley (p79)

**Granville Island**
HEIDI BESEN/SHUTTERSTOCK

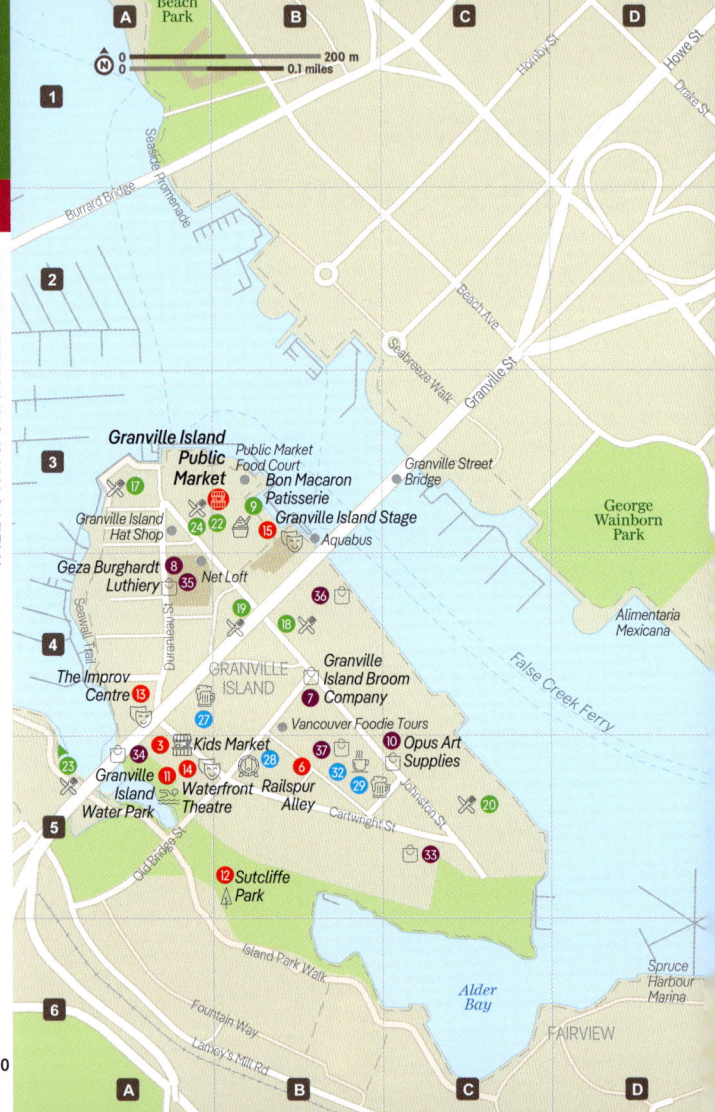

★ TOP EXPERIENCE

# Granville Island Public Market

One of North America's finest public markets, this food haven specializes in deli treats and pyramids of shiny fruit and vegetables. It is ideal for whiling away an afternoon, snacking in the sun among buskers on the patio or sheltering from rain inside on a guided market tour.

MAP P70 **B3**

**PLANNING TIP**
Arrive early to sidestep the summer crowds. If driving, weekdays are the easiest times to find on-island parking. If arriving by bike in summer, enjoy a complimentary bike-valet service.

Scan this QR code for a full list of shops.

### Foodie Tour

If you're looking for a local take on the food found around the famed market, a guided walk organized by **Vancouver Foodie Tours** *(foodietours.ca; $125)* is the way to go. This leisurely stomach-stuffer weaves around the vendors and includes several tasting stops that will quickly fill you up. It also caters to vegetarians if you mention it when you book. Should you be keen to carry on eating, the company runs tasting tours in other parts of the city too.

### Lee's Donuts

This mom-and-pop donut shop is legendary – just ask local celebrities like Seth Rogan who frequent the joint when they're in town. Serving handmade donuts since 1979, **Lee's Donuts** *(leesdonuts.ca)* offers a large variety of classics that are made daily from scratch (the sugar-topped raspberry jelly donut tops the list). Be sure to arrive early and expect a line – don't worry, though, the donuts are worth the wait.

### Mini Ferries

You can catch **Aquabus** *(theaquabus.com)* – a rainbow-colored mini pedestrian ferry – from the

MO WU/SHUTTERSTOCK

small dock found at the end of the boardwalk, behind the market. Take a short tour of the city afloat, or use the mini ferry to get to some of the city's best waterfront spots. Aquabus connects Granville Island with several scenic spots between downtown's Hornby St and Science World. Some mini ferries carry bikes.

## Net Loft

Found across the street, **Net Loft** is a sort of extension of the main market's artsy offerings. Here you'll find a cluster of craft shops that offer a variety of handcrafted keepsakes. At the nearby **Granville Island Hat Shop** *(thehatshop. ca)*, a small room packed to the rafters (literally) with hats from around the world, you can find everything from top hats to toques.

**QUICK BREAK**
Pop by the patio, painted in bright colors and scattered with straw umbrellas, at **Alimentaria Mexicana** to sip margaritas and dig into bold Mexican flavors.

## Boardwalk Buskers

A park-bench picnic behind the market is a preferred pastime for Granville Island locals and visiting tourists. Snack on treats collected during your stroll through the food stalls, and sit by the water, watching seagulls swoop (be sure to keep your food close or it might get snagged), while listening to talented buskers (pictured) perform live music. In Granville Island, busking is done through a licensed program, allowing everyone from magicians to musicians to showcase their talents on site. Check updated schedules and locations online before you go (granvilleislandbuskers.com).

## Arts & Crafts

There's a cool arts-and-crafts focus in Granville Island, especially among the collection of day vendors that dot the market and change every week.

**BRIDGE BIRDS**
Look up as you walk through Granville Island to the steelwork found under Granville Street Bridge. Pelagic cormorants often nest here, choosing the bridge's beams as their unlikely urban perch.

DGU/SHUTTERSTOCK

Hand-knitted hats, hand-painted ceramics, framed art photography and quirky carvings will make for excellent one-of-a-kind keepsakes. Further artisan stands are added to the roster in the run-up to Christmas, if you happen to be visiting at that time. For an updated list of day vendors that appear at the market, check out granvilleisland.com/public-market.

## Food Court

In the unlikely event that you're still hungry after snacking your way through the market stalls, there's also a small **Public Market Food Court** filled with varied offerings from around the world. Opt for off-peak dining if you want to snag a table and indulge in a good-value selection running from Mexican tacos to German sausages.

## Twin Bridges

If you're out enjoying the buskers on the market's waterfront exterior, you'll notice your False Creek view is sandwiched between two of Vancouver's most famous bridges. Opened in 1954, the ironwork **Granville Street Bridge** is the third version of this bridge to span the inlet here. The more attractive art-deco **Burrard Street Bridge** is nearby. During the bridge's opening ceremony in 1932, a floatplane was daringly piloted under its main deck.

**FORGOTTEN PAST**

Granville Island Public Market is one of Canada's most impressive urban-regeneration projects. Originally built as a factory district, the abandoned sheds attracted artists and theater groups by the 1970s. New theaters and studios were built and the public market became a popular anchor tenant. Now, only independent businesses operate here.

# WALKING TOUR

# Granville Island Artisan Amble

Most visitors head straight for Granville Island Public Market, but locals know there's more to this artificial island, built from sandbanks in False Creek over a century ago. Industrial sheds now house crafty shops, studio spaces and theaters, inviting leisurely waterfront exploration on sun-soaked days.

| START | END | LENGTH |
|---|---|---|
| Granville Island Licorice Parlour | Granville Island Brewing | 1km; one hour |

## 1 Licorice Love

Every stroll needs fuel, so drop into the friendly **Granville Island Licorice Parlour** (p83) for a hand-picked array of sweet and salty treats to keep you going. The free-standing candy shop has 90 different kinds of licorice, plus hula hoops and more.

## 2 Kids Only

There's more than one market on the island and this one is fully focused on the children. At **Kids Market** (p78), look out for wooden toys, well-curated books and a magic shop. Kids can also pop in for a play in the Adventure Zone.

## 3 Art Lovers Alley

Starting just outside the saloon-like Liberty Distillery, artisan-lined **Railspur Alley** (p79) is a haven of creative businesses. Look out for inventive hats, eye-popping paintings and fun fashions. This is also a great spot to stop for a coffee break.

## 4 Sake Sampling

In the middle of Railspur Alley, the **Artisan Sake Maker** (p82) – Canada's first sake winery – is a welcoming little storefront where you can sample unique Vancouver-made sake. Sample Japanese snacks, and even sake ice cream, and then snag a bottle to bring home.

## 5 Sweet Stop

Sample small-batch, handcrafted, bean-to-bar chocolates at **Kasama Chocolates** (p83), created by four friends looking to share unique flavors derived from cacao pods sourced in the Philippines.

## 6 Craft Central

A cluster of craft shops offers handcrafted keepsakes inside **Net Loft** (p73). Browse an expansive collection of beads (Swarovski crystals to bone beads) at **Beadworks** to create your own original piece of jewelry to take home. Net Loft's most popular store, **Paper-Ya** (p83), sells an irresistible array of hip stationary, quirky books and must-have art prints.

## 7 Market Shop

Dominating the island's busy end, **Granville Island Public Market** (p72) is a browser's paradise. If you're hungry, you can also dive into its tempting deli and bakery food stands. Arrive early to avoid long lines for fresh, handmade doughnuts at **Lee's Donuts** (p72).

## 8 Cheers with Beers!

Toast your wander in the taproom of one of Vancouver's oldest breweries, **Granville Island Brewing** (p82). Or take the guided tour, with samples included.

## EXPERIENCES

### See a Historic Train at Engine 374 Pavilion  TRAIN

The very first transcontinental passenger train trundled into Vancouver, linking the country by train from coast to coast and kickstarting the eventual metropolis, on May 23, 1887. The Canadian Pacific Railway locomotive that pulled this groundbreaking train – Engine 374 – was retired in 1945. After many years of neglect, it was restored and placed in the splendid **Engine 374 Pavilion** (MAP: ❶ P70 G3; *roundhouse.ca; free),* next to the **Roundhouse Community Arts & Recreation Centre** (MAP: ❷ P70 G2) in the heart of the city. Administered by the West Coast Railway Heritage Park in Squamish (a good excursion for rail buffs), the engine is kept in sparkling condition and is occasionally wheeled out onto the outside turntable for better viewing on warmer days. Friendly volunteers share railroading stories from yesteryear and show you the best angle for snapping photos of the historic engine.

### Shop For Toys  SHOPPING
MAP: ❸ P70 A5

Found adjacent to the entrance to Granville Island, beside a picturesque pond, **Kids Market** *(kidsmarket.ca)* is a three-story, warehouse-style shopping center aimed at kids. The yellow-hued building is topped with a rainbow sign, and with over 25 shops and services on site, it is an irresistible invitation to youngsters to shop, eat and play. You'll find handcrafted toys, locally owned boutiques and bookstores, interactive arcades, multi-level play spaces, and sweet-and-savory snack spots to fuel up after a day of play. Be sure to check out the website for year-round family-friendly events.

### Catch a Game  SPORTS
MAP: ❹ P70 H2

Also used for international rugby tournaments, rock concerts and consumer shows, the **BC Place Stadium** *(bcplace.com)* – with its huge, crown-like retractable roof – played host to the opening and closing ceremonies of the 2010 Olympic and Paralympic Winter Games. Vancouver's main sports arena, it is home to two professional teams: the **BC Lions** *(bclions.com)* Canadian Football League team and the **Vancouver Whitecaps** *(whitecapsfc.com)* soccer team. Single-game tickets are sold online via their official sites (or Ticketmaster), with prices kicking off at $25 or $30, depending on the match and seat locations.

### See Sports Relics  MUSEUM
MAP: ❺ P70 H2

Inside BC Place Stadium, you'll find the **BC Sports Hall of Fame & Museum** *(bcsportshall.com; adult/child $20/12).* This expertly curated attraction showcases top

BC athletes, both amateur and professional, with an intriguing array of galleries crammed with fascinating memorabilia. There are medals, trophies and yesteryear sports uniforms on display – judging by the size of their shirts, hockey players were much smaller in the past. There are also tons of hands-on activities to tire the kids out. Don't miss the **Indigenous Sport Gallery**, covering everything from hockey and lacrosse to traditional Indigenous games. Note the museum is closed on Mondays and also during stadium events; check it's open before visiting.

### See Artists in Action ARTS

Granville Island is packed with creative curiosities for art enthusiasts of all types. Stroll through **Railspur Alley** (MAP: ❻ P70 **B5**) to watch artists create masterpieces before your very eyes. See glassblowers, jewelers, potters, painters, blacksmiths and carvers craft beautiful pieces live in-studio and listen as they share the inspiration behind their work. Around the corner at **Granville Island Broom Company** (MAP: ❼ P70 **B4**; *broomcompany. com*), watch two sisters handcraft Shaker-style woven brooms in their whimsical storefront. Or visit the **Geza Burghardt Luthiery** (MAP: ❽ P70 **A4**; *gezaburghardt.com*) to learn how Hungarian luthier Geza Burghardt builds, repairs and restores guitars, violins, cellos and other string instruments.

### Get Crafty ART CLASS

Don't just watch artists from afar – get hands-on with a crafty art or baking class. Satisfy your sweet tooth while mastering the art of macaron-making with a private class at **Bon Macaron Patisserie** (MAP: ❾ P70 **B3**; *bonmacaronpatisserie.com; 3hr workshop $95*). Originally from France, the owners bring unique flavors to classic French pastrymaking. From candied pecan, to blue cheese and pear, you'll want to buy an assorted box when leaving so you can try them all at home.

Or sign up for an in-store painting class at **Opus Art Supplies** (MAP: ❿ P70 **C5**; *opusartsupplies. com; from $45*), a spacious store that is a staple of the Vancouver art community. Here you'll find everything from professional-grade paints, brushes, canvases and papers to framing supplies, art books and specialty tools. Not only can you tap into your creative side, you can make something to bring home as a keepsake.

### Spray, Splash and Slide at the Granville Island Water Park PARK

Kids love to splash, spray and slide at the largest, free outdoor water park of its kind in North America. With its fire hydrants, in-ground sprays, fountains and a twirly yellow slide, **Granville Island Water Park** (MAP: ⓫ P70 **A5**; *falsecreekcc.ca/waterpark; free*) is the perfect summer cool-down

### BEST PERFORMING ARTS VENUES
A trio of live-performance venues form Granville Island's theater district *(gitd.ca)*, the best 'hood for theater, improv and performing arts.

#### The Improv Centre
MAP: **13** P70 **A4**
Known for its high-energy, unscripted comedy, featuring shows like *The Late Show*, *Theatresports* and seasonal favorite *Scared Scriptless*.

#### Waterfront Theatre
MAP: **14** P70 **A5**
Intimate space hosting plays, festivals, community productions, performances during the Vancouver Fringe Festival *(vancouverfringe. com)* and events by Carousel Theatre for Young People.

#### Granville Island Stage
MAP: **15** P70 **B3**
A 440-seat venue run by the Arts Club Theatre Company *(artsclub. com)*. Enjoy professional productions like *Made in Italy* and *The Birds and the Bees*.

for kids. Slather on the sunscreen and enjoy the splash pads. Then pick up some snacks from the Granville Island Public Market – a short walk from the park – and settle down in the expansive grassy green space and kids' playground of adjacent **Sutcliffe Park** (MAP: **12** P70 **B5**).

### Picnic in the Park    PARK
MAP: **16** P70 **F3**
The main draw of waterfront **David Lam Park** is its large grassy space with the city's skyscrapers and water views as dramatic backdrop. But little kids love the swings and slides in the park's playground too. The green space is sometimes used for free alfresco summer movie screenings. It's an ideal launch point for a seawall walk along the north bank of False Creek to Science World; you'll pass intriguing public artworks and the glass condo towers that transformed the neighborhood in the 1990s along the way. And if a quiet picnic is more your speed, this is a great spot for that too.

# LISTINGS

# Best Places for...

$ Budget  $$ Midrange  $$$ Top End

## Eating

**Alfresco Dining**

### Tap & Barrel Bridges $$
**17** A3

This bright-yellow waterfront landmark sports one of Vancouver's best sunset patios from which to enjoy (slightly pricey) pub-style dishes like fish and chips or beef short ribs. *tapandbarrel.com; 11am-11pm Mon-Thu, to midnight Fri, 10am-midnight Sat, to 10pm Sun*

### Sandbar $$
**18** B4

West Coast seafood dominates at this slick, high-ceilinged restaurant-with-view near Granville Bridge. The popular fresh oysters are best sampled on the fireplace-warmed rooftop deck. *vancouverdine.com/sandbar; 11:30am-10:30pm Mon-Fri, from 11am Sat & Sun*

### Alimentaria Mexicana $$
**19** B4

This lively Mexican cantina lures in punters with its colorful corner patio and tasty crispy cauliflower tacos, *carnitas torta* with chorizo and cinnamon-scented house-made churros. *alimentariamexicana.com; 11:30am-9:30pm Sun-Thu, to 10:30pm Fri & Sat*

### Dockside Restaurant $$
**20** C5

Inside Granville Island Hotel, this spot is best known for its harbor-front patio and superb seafood. Inside is charming too with its open kitchen and a 50ft aquarium. *docksidevancouver.com; 7:30am-9:30pm, to 10:30pm Fri & Sat*

### Blue Water Cafe $$
**21** G1

Consistently recognized as Vancouver's best seafood restaurant, Blue Water Cafe serves up fine West Coast–inspired cuisine in a refurbished brick-and-beam warehouse. The Raw Bar offers fresh sushi and sashimi. *bluewatercafe.ca; 4:30-10:30pm Sun-Thu, to 11:30pm Fri & Sat*

**See p70** for map of locations

**Casual Eats**

### Lee's Donuts $
**22** B3

Serving fresh, handmade classic donuts since 1979, Lee's has become a top spot for donuts in the city. As you stroll around Granville Island, spot the bright yellow boxes in the hands of passersbys. *leesdonuts.ca; 8am-7pm*

### Go Fish $
**23** A5

A short stroll westward along the seawall from the Granville Island entrance, this seafood stand is a favorite fish-and-chip joint. Halibut, salmon and cod come encased in crispy golden batter. *11:30am-7pm Tue-Fri, from noon Sat*

### A Bread Affair $
**24** A3

A must-visit for fans of great bread. Alongside a sandwich bar and racks of freshly baked organic loaves, there's an irresistible array of sweet treats: cookies, croissants, rich chocolate brownies and more. *abreadaffair.com; 9am-9pm Mon-Thu, to 6:30pm Fri-Sun*

### Rodney's Oyster House $$

 F2

The folks at this pilgrimage spot for oysters know how to do seafood. While the freshly shucked oysters with a huge array of sauces (try the spicy vodka) impress every time, dishes like chunky chowders and sautéed garlic shrimp are also served. *rohvan.com; 3pm-11pm, to midnight Fri & Sat, from noon Sat & Sun*

### Fine Dining

### Elisa $$$

26 G1

Elegant steakhouse with elevated dishes, Michelin-recognized for its BC-sourced meats, Japanese wagyu and beef Wellington among other top-choice cuts. Dungeness crab spring rolls are a must-try starter. *elisasteak.com; 4:30pm-midnight*

# Drinking

## Beer & Spirits

### Granville Island Brewing Taproom

27 A4

In this often busy pub-style room, sample the brewery's main beers like the cypress honey lager. Or opt for the small-batch brews made right here on the island; ask the server what's available. *granvilleislandbrewing.ca; 11am-9pm Sun-Thu, to 10pm Fri & Sat*

### Liberty Distillery

28 B5

Gaze through internal windows at the shiny, steampunk-like booze-making equipment inside this handsome saloon-style tasting room. During happy hour (3pm–6pm & after 8pm Mon-Thu) sample house-made vodka, gins and whiskeys. *thelibertydistillery.com; hours vary*

### Artisan Sake Maker

 B5

Using locally grown rice, this tiny craft sake producer (the first of its kind in Canada) is worth a visit. Sake maker Masa Shiroki creates tempting tipples that you can dive into with a bargain $5 three-sake tasting. *artisansakemaker.com; 11:30am-6pm*

## Coffee Shops

### Small Victory

30 G1

This granite-countered coffee shop is a favorite daytime hangout for hip Yaletowners. Consume your cappuccino and flaky croissant (there's also an artful array of other bakery treats) under the geometric wall-mounted artwork and you'll fit right in. *smallvictory.ca; 8am-5pm*

### Matchstick

31 E2

Tucked into the bottom of a shimmering glass condo building, this cool coffee shop has friendly staff, excellent coffee and irresistible sweet treats and hearty sandwiches. Go for the tuna melt. *matchstickyvr.com; 7am-5pm, closed Mon*

### Off the Tracks

 B5

This slightly hidden cafe on Railspur Alley is a popular coffee stop with good-value all-day breakfasts. Lunch delivers soups, salads, sandwiches and wraps, and there's also BC craft beer. *tracksbistro.ca; 9am-5pm Sun-Thu, to 6pm Fri & Sat*

# Shopping

## Sweet Treats

### Kasama Chocolates
**33** C5

For a take-home sweet treat, head here for bean-to-bar chocolate and truffles made using unique ingredients. The durian chocolate bar is made from the namesake pungent tropical fruit, widely grown across Southeast Asia. *kasamachocolate.com; 10am-5pm Wed-Fri & Sun, to 6pm Sat*

### Granville Island Licorice Parlour
**34** A5

This sweet-tooth candy spot serves up dozens of jars of serious licorice alongside a kaleidoscopic mix of sweeties and bonbons like jelly babies and saltwater taffy. *facebook.com/licoriceparlour; 10am-6pm*

## Arts & Crafts

### Paper-Ya
**35** A4

This store's treasure trove of trinkets ranges from natty pens to traditional washi paper. There's also a changing roster of hard-to-resist goodies like cool journals, quirky books and cute greeting cards. *paper-ya.com; 10am-6pm*

### Opus Art Supplies
see **10** C5

This store is like a candy shop for creatives, packed with pastels, paints and every kind of paper, as well as framing, fine art and card printing. Look out for regular demos and workshops. *opusartsupplies.com; 10am-6pm*

### Silk Weaving Studio
**36** B4

This working studio and textiles shop is a crafter's delight – it's hard not to stroke every strand of silk, threads and yarns in sight, such is the rainbow of color. Watch for weaving demonstrations. *silkweavingstudio.com; 10am-5pm*

## Women's Fashions

### Allison Wonderland Atelier
**37** B5

The colorful and cozy pieces here are uniquely designed, locally made, and often inspired by the 70s. The chic pieces fit, flatter and feel good. Browse cases of colorful jewelry too. *allisonwonderland.ca; 11am-5pm*

### Fine Finds
**38** H1

Browse racks of carefully curated independent labels at this locally owned women's fashion boutique, and try not to take everything home. It also showcases the work of local jewelry designers and artists. *finefindsboutique.com; 11am-6pm*

## Gifts & Homewares

### Cross Decor & Design
**39** G2

Housed in a heritage building, this home-goods store is all about the appealing aesthetic. Often referred to as a 'home decor fantasy land,' it sells a wide range of furniture, textiles, accessories and gifts. *thecrossdesign.com; 10am-6pm Mon-Sat, 11am-5pm Sun*

### Portobello West
**40** G3

This arts, crafts and fashion market runs once each season in the Roundhouse building. Expect to find an eclectic mix of handmade, one-of-a-kind goodies and locally designed keepsakes. Enjoy live music and food-truck treats too. *portobellowest.com; 10am-5pm*

**See p92** for eating, drinking and shopping listings

# Explore
# Main St & Mt Pleasant

Named one of North America's coolest streets, the formerly faded neighborhood of Main St is now a hipster hub. It is home to numerous independent shops, global restaurants and trendy bars, all within a 20-block stretch. The area is developing rapidly, including the lower Olympic Village area – a waterfront neighborhood that's always evolving. Some of the city's best restaurants, including a handful of Michelin-recognized spots, are found in this area. The dining scene is culturally diverse, offering a mix of laid-back and high-end addresses serving up everything from Malaysian and South Indian to Caribbean classics.

## Getting Around

### 🚆 SkyTrain
The Skytrain takes you to the base of this neighborhood, with a stop just steps from Science World and Olympic Village.

### 🚌 Bus
Stroll up the Main St strip for murals and vintage shops, or take a bus. Services run regularly throughout the day.

### 🚗 Rideshare
Easily accessible from this central location, Rideshare assures a quick trip back to your home base.

### 🚶 On Foot
Once in situ, the area is walkable and easy to navigate with flat, well-marked streets.

★
**THE BEST**

**ATTRACTION FOR KIDS**
Science World (p87)

**STREET MURAL** The Present Is a Gift (p89)

**ARCHITECTURAL SITE**
Heritage Hall (p91)

**MICHELIN MEAL** Burdock & Co (p92)

**URBAN PARK** Creekside Park (p90)

**Heritage Hall (p91)**
MICHAEL WHEATLEY/ALAMY

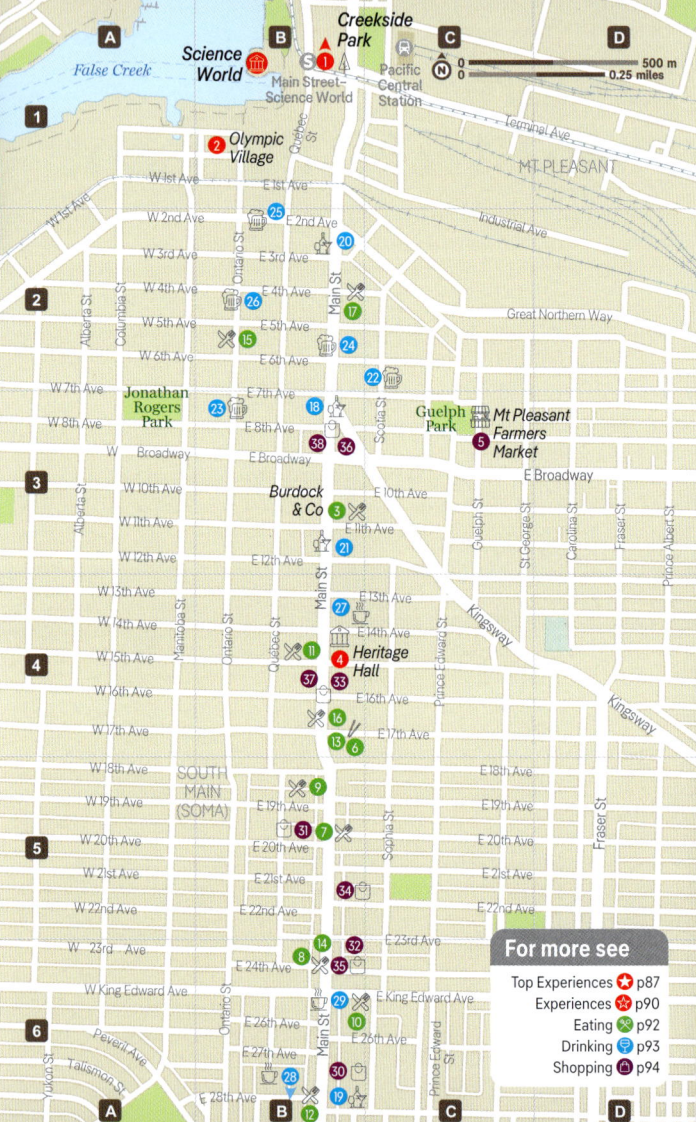

## ★ TOP EXPERIENCE

# Science World

One of the city's most photographed structures, this dome isn't just a shiny shoreline bauble: **Science World** *(scienceworld. ca; adult/child $35/24)* assures fun for all ages. Educational play areas, hands-on exhibits and science demos fill two floors.

MAP P86 **B1**

### Ground-Floor Fun
Let your kids loose in the **Puzzles & Illusions Gallery**, a tactile array of activities with wobble rings and whisper dishes. Check out the schedule of live science demonstrations happening multiple times a day at the nearby Centre Stage.

### Upstairs Discoveries
Next, wander up to the second level, encircled by themed galleries packed with hands-on action, including the nature-focused **Search: Sara Stern Gallery** (with fossils, taxidermy and live critters) and the brilliant **BodyWorks**, exploring the engineering marvels of the human body, with every fascinating function fully explained. The **Eureka Gallery** is a hit with little kids (book extra time for play at the water table). Pop into the **Science Theatre** to enjoy short films.

### Outdoor Play
In fine weather, save time for the outdoor **Ken Spencer Science Park**, open mid-March to early November. Focused on connecting with nature, this huge outdoor gallery features climbing frames, rugged interactive games, stage demonstrations and a 'What's in your lunchbox' garden exhibit. Say hello to resident hens, and visit Science World's gift shop on your way out.

**PLANNING TIP**
Arrive closer to opening and aim for a weekday visit. To avoid long lines, plan ahead and buy tickets online. Same-day tickets, however, can only be purchased in-person.

Scan this QR code for tickets, exhibits, films and events.

# WALKING TOUR

# Metropolitan Mural Meander

View some of Vancouver's 300-plus vibrant murals in 11 neighborhoods, a lasting legacy of the yesteryear Vancouver Mural Festival. A stroll along this Main St stretch unveils bold art on streets, alleys and building facades. The Astro Arts Festival (astroarts.ca) celebrates urban art in the city today.

| START | END | LENGTH |
|---|---|---|
| Snapshots of History | Waggle Dance | 4km; 50 minutes |

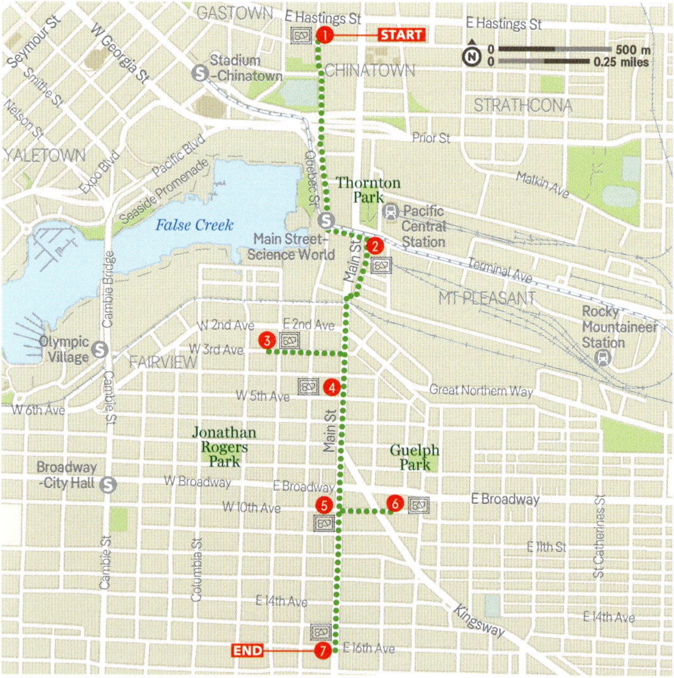

### ❶ Piecing Together the Past
Start on the edge of Chinatown with a look at **Snapshots of History** (490 Columbia St), a mural inviting reflection on Chinese-Canadian heritage and capturing key moments in early Chinese-Canadian life. It highlights both personal stories – such as the Goon family's struggle against discrimination – and historical street scenes reflecting the community's resilience and contribution.

### ❷ Honoring The Land
Stop by **Listening. On. Waking Terrain.** (220 Terminal Ave) by Indigenous artist Bracken Hanuse Corlett (Wuikinuxv and Klahoose Nations). The mural blends traditional Indigenous art with digital media to honor the land's history and first peoples. Fittingly placed on Vancouver's first modular housing site, it reflects loss, resilience, connection and hope.

### ❸ Forging Ahead
Make your way along Quebec St and stop at **Entangled Flow** (31 W 3rd Ave). The mural forms part of the city's so-called Climate Collection, addressing themes relating to climate change, environmental justice and sustainability. This piece looks at the entanglement of environment and society, how to heal damage, and forging a new path for Earth's future.

### ❹ Craving Attention
Duck into a side alley on Main St to admire **Thirsty** (2015 Main St) by Vancouver-based street artist iHeart, also known as I♥. The stencil of a young girl holding a phone is a critique on society's obsession with digital approval and the emotional thirst created by online culture, and provokes reflection on modern connection.

### ❺ Living In The Moment
Stand on E Broadway to spot the massive **The Present Is a Gift** (2543 Main St). This portrait mural parallels two Mt Pleasant residents: born-and-bred Paisley Nahanee of the Coast-Salish First Nations, and community optometrist Dr Bob who has worked locally for over six decades.

### ❻ Finding Connection
Continue up Main St to 10th Ave to unearth **Ode to the Oceans** (350 E 10th Ave). This striking street art serves as a powerful reminder that vibrant marine life thrives in the ocean surrounding the city, and assures the natural beauty and ecological health of the Pacific Northwest region.

### ❼ Buzzing Ahead
End with **Waggle Dance** (3207 Main St), a vibrant mural celebrating the vital role of honeybees. The detailed image depicts their fascinating 'waggle dance', a hive ritual that guides other bees to the richest nectar sources.

## EXPERIENCES

### Play at Creekside Park — PARK
MAP: ❶ P86 **B1**

A popular outdoor venue for summer events and festivals and the gateway to Science World, **Creekside Park** is also home to Vancouver's largest playground. The accessible play area features a high-reaching wooden climbing tower, swings, giant tube and hill slides, musical instruments, water and sand play areas, and a play hut – all on a colorful rubberized surface. Adding extra zest to the park's fun features is a zipline – perhaps the biggest draw. Trees around the park's perimeter provide shaded seating areas, perfect for picnics. Waterfront and skyline views naturally attract park visitors without kids too.

### Spend the Day at Olympic Village — VILLAGE

Originally built to house athletes for the 2010 Winter Olympic and Paralympic Games, Vancouver's **Olympic Village** (MAP: ❷ P86 **B1**) has now evolved into a happening spot, packed with pubs, patios and waterfront parks. Look for *The Birds,* a pair of giant sparrows by local artist Myfanwy MacLeod – standing 18ft tall in the center of the square, the scultural ensemble is hard to miss. The artwork comments on the relationship between humans and birds, and the effects of urban development in a formerly natural space.

Be sure to cross **Canoe Bridge** (a popular photo spot), which is especially beautiful when illuminated at night. Steps away, you'll find **Sole Food Street Farms**, an urban farm and social enterprise. Produce here ends up on plates at restaurants like Michelin-starred **Burdock & Co** (MAP: ❸ P86 **B3**). Be sure to visit the weekly farmers' market, held here on Wednesdays.

### Indulge in a Michelin Meal — DINING

Mt Pleasant's 'Michelin Mile' runs along Main St – a stretch known for its concentration of acclaimed restaurants. Vancouver's first-ever Michelin guide was released in 2022 and, currently, 10 spots have received one-star recognition; another 15 have bib gourmand designation. Several others were also added to the esteemed list of restaurants in the city.

Dining options are definitely worth discovering, offering distinct dishes that showcase both the freshly plucked local ingredients found in the region (especially seafood), and the city's Asian influence, with many of the dishes found nowhere else outside Asia. Standout dishes – such as grilled cabbage with miso butter and dry-aged duck cooked up at Published on Main (p92) – blend Pacific Northwest ingredients with Japanese techniques. Be sure to book your table well in advance.

 **LITTLE ITALY**

Located just east of the Main St area and recognized as Vancouver's Little Italy, Commercial Drive or 'The Drive' was shaped by Italian immigrants in the 1950s and the counterculture movement of the 1960s. The renowned strip remains one of Vancouver's most eclectic and character-rich neighborhoods, packed with independent shops, vintage stores and cafes. And, of course, you'll find lots of espresso bars, trattorias and Italian butcher shops here too.

### Head to Heritage Hall
ARCHITECTURE

MAP: ❹ P86 **B4**

**Heritage Hall** (*heritagehall vancouver.ca*) has been an iconic landmark in the Mt Pleasant neighborhood since 1916. On the corner of Main St and 15th Ave, the stunning stone building topped with a clock tower was originally built as a post office. It has since become a hub for community events (think: comic book sales, public dance parties, pop-up shops, crafts fairs). The upper rooms double as office spaces for some local nonprofit organizations, and weddings and film shoots often fill the main ballroom (which can be rented). The building is worth a visit just for its exterior architecture, but do check its events calendar online too as there's invariably something fun happening inside.

### Visit Main St Markets
SHOPPING

MAP: ❺ P86 **C3**

Vancouverites love markets and there are many to keep them busy throughout the city. The **Mt Pleasant Farmers Market** that unfolds on Sunday mornings (10am to 2pm, May to October), in Dude Chilling Park (8th Ave & Guelph St) is perfect for picking up seasonal BC-grown peaches, blueberries and luscious cherries. While mulling over your produce options, there are usually more than a few baked treats to indulge in too. This is one of many markets organized by Vancouver Farmers Markets (*VFM; eatlocal. org*); check online for other locations.

Pop-up craft markets make a regular appearance around the city. **Made in the 604** (*madeinthe604. ca*) lands in various city spots in spring and summer; it's often hosted at Heritage Hall. Check its events page for times and locations.

## LISTINGS

# Best Places for...

**$** Budget  **$$** Midrange  **$$$** Top End

**See p86** for map of locations

## Eating

### Michelin Meals

**Anh & Chi $$**
 B4

This vibrant Vietnamese is backed by a brother-and-sister team who embrace their culinary roots, producing authentic Vietnamese dishes like *khay bánh hỏi lụi nướng,* a DIY streetside platter served with a modern twist. *anhandchi.com; 11am-11pm*

**Published on Main $$$**
 B5

Executive chef Gus Stieffenhofer-Brandson and his team prepare picture-perfect dishes using ingredients, some foraged, from farms and local forests. The food is high-quality, and the presentation, impressive. The tender halibut with buttery broth is a crowd pleaser. *publishedonmain.com; 5-11pm*

**Burdock & Co $$$**
see  B3

With Andrea Carlson, the only female chef on Vancouver's Michelin list, at the helm, this popular spot is best known for its seasonal set-course menu made up of regional farm-to-table plates. *5-10pm Thu-Mon*

**Acorn $$$**
 B6

One of Vancouver's hottest vegetarian restaurants, the Acorn is ideal for those craving something more inventive than veggie soup. Consider seasonal, artfully presented treats like beer-battered haloumi or vanilla-almond-beet cake. *theacornrestaurant.ca; 5:30-11:30pm Mon-Fri, 10am-2pm Sat & Sun*

**Suyo Modern Peruvian $$$**
 B5

Served in a plant-filled dining room, the food here is sophisticated but unfussy. Modern Peruvian dishes are the focus, with ceviche, *lomo saltado* and *anticuchos* being some of the more popular picks. *suyo.ca; 5-9:30pm Tue-Sun*

### Casual Eats

**Sula Indian Restaurant $$**
 B6

Savor South Indian-inspired cuisine featuring traditional roast coconut-based curries and distinctive Mumbai street foods. *sulaindianrestaurant.com; hours vary*

**Burgoo Bistro $$**
 B4

Internationally-inspired comfort foods and a tasty weekend brunch menu are served in a rustic-chic shack with buzzing summer patio. *burgoo.ca; 11am-10pm*

**East is East $$**
 B6

Indian and Middle Eastern flavors meet live music, dance and the city's best chai. Visit weekdays for smaller crowds. *eastiseast.ca; 11:30am-10pm Sun-Thu, to 11pm Fri & Sat*

### Good Thief $$
 B4

This casual sister spot to Michelin-recognized Ahn & Chi serves elevated Vietnamese bites and an innovative cocktail menu. *goodthief.ca; 5-11pm Sun-Thu, to midnight Fri & Sat*

### Lila $$
 B6

Modern Indian cuisine, best enjoyed family-style, paired with a thoughtful collection of cocktails. Dine on the hidden patio. *lilarestaurant.ca; 5-10pm Mon-Fri, noon-10pm Sat & Sun*

### Tacofino Ocho $$
 B2

The eighth location of the Vancouver mini-chain serves up tasty tacos and mezcal in a cool, industrial-style space in Mt Pleasant. *tacofino.com; 11:30am-10pm Sun-Thu, to 11pm Fri & Sat*

### El Camino's $$
 B4

Enjoy Latin American street food in this casual cantina, with a buzzing patio and lively atmosphere. *elcaminos.ca; hours vary*

### Zarak by Afghan Kitchen $$
 B2

Generational Afghan recipes served alongside modern takes, with a cocktail menu inspired by family stories and cultural heritage. The space is stylish yet welcoming, with a relaxed atmosphere that suits both casual meals and special occasions. *zarakvancouver.com; hours vary*

## Drinking

### Cocktail Spots

### Key Party
 B3

Walk through the doorway of a fake storefront resembling an accountancy office to uncover this candlelit, boudoir-red speakeasy with an entertaining cocktail program. Kir royale jello shooters! *keyparty.ca; 5pm-1am Mon-Thu & Sun, to 2am Fri & Sat*

### Shameful Tiki Room
 B6

This windowless spot transports you to a Polynesian beach. Tiki masks and rattan coverings line walls beneath a straw-shrouded ceiling. But it's the drinks that rock: well-crafted classics from blue Hawaiis to a four-person volcano bowl. *shamefultikiroom.com; 5pm-midnight Sun-Thu, to 1am Fri & Sat*

### Narrow Lounge
 B2

Enter the doorway on 3rd Ave, then descend the graffiti-lined stairway into one of Vancouver's coolest small bars. Lined with taxidermy and junk-shop pictures, it's an atmospheric nook. In summer, try the hidden alfresco bar out back. *narrowlounge.com; 5pm-1am Mon-Thu, 4pm-2am Fri-Sun*

### Sing Sing Beer Bar
 B3

This bright, white-walled, plant-accented bar would look at home on a Singapore side street. Snag a communal table and dive into 20 or so BC craft-beer taps. On the menu: an unusual combination of pizzas and hearty pho bowls. *freehouse.co; 11:30am-1am Sun-Thu, to 2am Fri & Sat*

### Breweries

### Main St Brewing
 C2

Tucked into a historic, yellow-painted brewery building, Main St Brewing has a chatty, industrial-chic tasting room and a booze roster divided into regular beers and seasonal casks. *mainstreetbeer.ca;*

noon-10pm Mon-Thu, to 11pm Fri & Sat, to 9:30pm Sun

### 33 Acres Brewing Company
23 B3

A staple in the Brewery Creek district, this popular spot is known for its craft beer and community focus. True beer buffs should check out its 33 Brewing Experiment bar next door, with up to 20 taps pouring test and small-batch brews. *33acresbrewing.com; noon-11pm Sun-Thu, to midnight Fri & Sat*

### Brassneck Brewery
24 B2

This beloved microbrewery has a small, wood-lined tasting room. Peruse the ever-changing chalkboard of intriguing libations with names like Pinky Promise, Silent Treatment and Faux Naive. Consider starting with a Passive Aggressive dry-hopped pale ale. *brassneck.ca; 2-11pm Tue-Fri, to 10pm Sun & Mon, open 12pm Sat*

### Brewhall
25 B2

A modern-day reinvention of Bavarian beer halls, this cavernous heritage building serves own-made beers, plus drafts from top BC microbreweries. Order drinks and pick up at the bar (the Neon Lights pale ale is recommended), then decamp to a chatty long table. *brewhall.com; 11:30am-midnight*

### Electric Bicycle Brewing
26 B2

Behind its eye-popping psychedelic facade, this quirky little brewery tasting room has a kitsch ice-cream parlour feel. Dive into a four-glass flight of house-made beers, from kölsch to sours, and you'll soon be in the groove. *electricbicyclebrewing.com; noon-10pm Sun-Thu, to midnight Fri & Sat*

## Coffee Shops

### 49th Parallel Coffee Roasters
27 B4

Housed in a large, brick-lined hangout, routinely crammed with locals. Sustainably sourced and crafted coffee roasted locally, with an exceptional selection of donuts. *49thcoffee.com; 7am-6pm*

### Matchstick Coffee
28 B6

Bright, airy and open, the Main St location of this popular local coffee chain is a great community space packed with locals. Snag a spot at the shared wooden long table, and snack on a delicious croissant with your caffeinated bevy. *matchstickvr.com; 7am-5pm Wed-Mon*

### Aperture Coffee Bar
29 B6

A cozy, moto-themed cafe with a warm wood decor and jazzy evening vibe. Satisfy your sweet tooth with an affogato flight, or lunch on a spicy tuna sandwich. *aperturecoffeebar.com; 8am-9:30pm*

# Shopping

## Specialty Shops

### Red Cat Records
30 B6

Arguably Vancouver's coolest record store. It has a brilliantly curated collection of new and used vinyl and CDs, and is co-owned by musicians; ask them for tips on where to see great local acts. *redcat.ca; 11:30am-6:30pm Sun-Fri, from 10:30am Sat*

### Neptoon Records
**31** B5

Vancouver's oldest independent record store is still a major lure for music fans. You'll find a well-priced array of new and used vinyl and CDs, plus some serious help with finding that obscure record you've been looking for. *neptoon.com; 11am-6:30pm*

### Regional Assembly of Text
**32** B6

Journals, handmade pencil boxes and T-shirts printed with typewriter motifs lure locals. Check out the tiny under-the-stairs gallery, and don't miss the monthly Letter Writing Club (7pm first Thursday of month) when you can type on vintage typewriters. *assemblyoftext.com; 11am-6pm Mon-Sat, noon-5pm Sun*

### Urban Source
**33** B4

From used postcards and insect rubber stamps to ladybug stickers and map pages from old books, this brilliant store offers a highly eclectic, ever-changing array of reclaimed materials and alternative arts-and-crafts supplies. *urban-source.ca; 10:30am-5:30pm Mon-Sat, from 11am Sun*

### Front & Company
**34** B5

This is the ideal store to pick up a quirky souvenir for that difficult person back home who hates maple syrup (does such a person exist?); buy something cool for yourself while you're at it. *frontandcompany.ca; 11am-6:30pm*

### Lucky's Books & Comics
**35** B6

Don't be put off by the unassuming, windowless exterior of this local favorite. Instead, nip inside for a cornucopia of esoteric storybooks, graphic novels, oddball zines and homemade chapbooks at one of Vancouver's coolest independent stores. *luckys.ca; 11am-6pm Sat-Thu, to 7pm Fri*

## Vintage & Consignment
### Mintage Mall
**36** B3

Comprising seven super-cool vintage vendors offering everything from 1970s outfits (at Thirteen Moons) to antique taxidermy (Salamander Salt Curio), this eclectic, labyrinthine upstairs 'mall' is one of the best ways to spend an hour in Mt Pleasant. *mintagevintage.com; 11am-7pm Mon-Sat, to 6pm Sun*

### Turnabout Luxury Resale
**37** B4

This well-stocked shop is stuffed with curated and consignment luxury fashions, footwear and finds. Since 1978, it has been the place to find those seemingly unattainable brand-name items (yes, even those Prada pumps) at an affordable price. *turnabout.com; 10am-6pm Mon-Sat, from noon Sun*

### F as in Frank
**38** B3

This large, fashion-forward vintage store stocks a kaleidoscope of wildly eclectic, original retro clothing, from 1970s concert T-shirts to 1990s grunge-wear. It has a particular penchant for yesteryear sportswear too. *fasinfrankvintage.com; noon-7pm Mon-Fri, from 11am Sat & Sun*

# Explore
# Fairview & South Granville

Combining the boutiques and restaurants of well-to-do South Granville with Fairview's busy Broadway thoroughfare and cozy Cambie Village, this area has something for everyone. South Granville is home to tree-lined residential streets, heritage buildings and casual cafes intermixed with modern boutiques and high-end eateries. A stretch of stylish shops and independent galleries make this vibrant, upscale shopping district worth the trek. Art lovers will want to walk along 'Gallery Row' – a stretch of art galleries that line the lower South Granville corridor. Green-thumbed visitors should also save time for some top-notch park and garden attractions here.

## Getting Around

 **Car**
Sights are more spread out in this neighborhood, so you may want to rent a car or consider Rideshare to see it all or venture to places further afield like Richmond.

 **Bus**
Regular buses run along Granville St to downtown, and further towards Queen Elizabeth Park or into Richmond.

 **On Foot**
The shops and galleries found along Granville Street are easily walkable between Broadway and West 16th, a seven-block stretch.

## THE BEST

**BOTANICAL GARDEN**
VanDusen Botanical Garden (p100)

**BIRD VIEWING** Bloedel Conservatory (p104)

**SPORTS VENUE** Nat Bailey Stadium (p104)

**INDIGENOUS CUISINE** Salmon n' Bannock (p105)

**HERITAGE THEATER** Stanley Theatre (p104)

**Caffé Barney (p106), South Granville**
JOHN MITCHELL/ALAMY

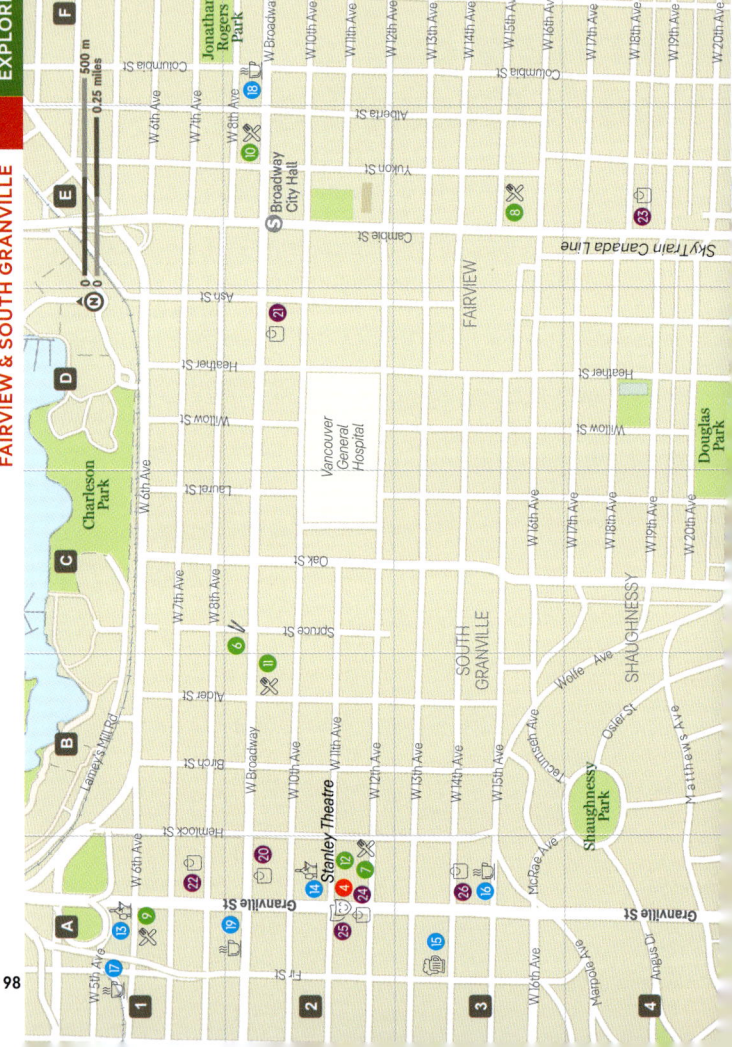

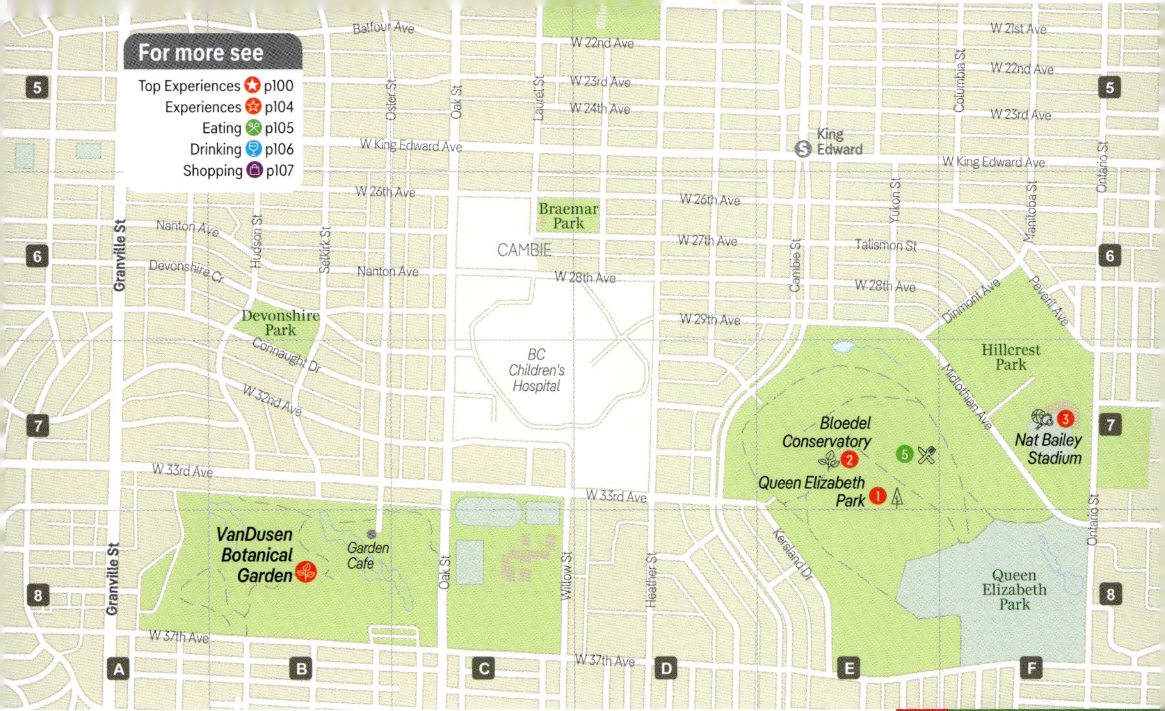
For more see
Top Experiences p100
Experiences p104
Eating p105
Drinking p106
Shopping p107
Balfour Ave
W 21st Ave
W 22nd Ave
W 23rd Ave
W 24th Ave
W King Edward Ave
King Edward
W 26th Ave
W 27th Ave
W 28th Ave
W 29th Ave
W 32nd Ave
W 33rd Ave
W 37th Ave
Nanton Ave
Devonshire Cr
Connaught Dr
Talisman St
Dinmont Ave
Peveril Ave
Midlothian Ave
Kersland Dr
Granville St
Hudson St
Selkirk St
Osler St
Oak St
Laurel St
Willow St
Heather St
Cambie St
Yukon St
Columbia St
Manitoba St
Ontario St
Braemar Park
CAMBIE
Devonshire Park
BC Children's Hospital
Hillcrest Park
Bloedel Conservatory
Queen Elizabeth Park
Nat Bailey Stadium
Queen Elizabeth Park
VanDusen Botanical Garden
Garden Cafe
1
2
3
5
A
B
C
D
E
F
5
6
7
8

## ⭐ TOP EXPERIENCE

# VanDusen Botanical Garden

Vancouver's favorite **garden** *(vandusengarden.org; adult/child $14/9)* is a plant lover's paradise, with leafy walkways lined with over 500 varieties of local and exotic flora, from temperate trees to tropical flowers. Get lost in the hedge maze, and look out for herons, owls and turtles that call the park home.

MAP P98 **B8**

**PLANNING TIP**
Be sure to stop and quiz the wandering volunteers: they are full of knowledge about the plants and wildlife you'll spot during your visit.

### Plant Life

Opened in 1975, this 22-hectare green-thumbed wonderland is home to more than 250,000 plants representing some of the world's most distinctive growing regions. Find trees, shrubs, flowers, succulents and more from across Canada, the Mediterranean, South Africa and the Himalayas. There's almost always something in bloom here; that might include the eye-popping **Rhododendron Walk** or the neon-yellow, tunnel-like **Laburnum Walk**. Pick up a self-guided tour sheet from the visitor center (pictured) for seasonal tips on what to see, or time your visit for a free guided tour.

### Wildlife

This sparkling nature spot is also a haven for wildlife. Seek out turtles, herons and ducks in and around the main lake. In quiet corners you might also see owls, bats, raccoons or the occasional coyote. But birds are the main critters here. There are regular guided bird walks (included with admission) and highlights include eagles, hummingbirds and woodpeckers. Pollinators love it here too.

### Elizabethan Maze

Grown from more than 3000 pyramidal cedars, VanDusen's giggle-triggering traditional maze is

Scan this QR code for a list of upcoming events.

STEPHANIE BRACONNIER/SHUTTERSTOCK

the perfect spot to tire out your kids. Alternatively, just send them in there alone while you take a break outside. Now more than 25 years old, the maze has just the right combination of confusing dead-ends and gratifying solvability to give most visitors an entertaining diversion.

## Garden Art

Sculptures and fountains dot the grounds. In 1975 the Vancouver International Stone Sculpture Symposium invited 12 international artists to produce 11 large stone sculptures with students from what is now known as the Emily Carr School of Art; they remain part of the garden's art collection. Other sculptures have been gifted or commissioned by the VanDusen Botanical Garden Association.

**QUICK BREAK**
Head to VanDusen's **Garden Cafe** for light lunch options, including handmade sandwiches, soups, curries and fair-trade coffee. Try for a patio table facing the garden.

# WALKING TOUR

# Walk South Granville

Stylish shops and independent galleries make this upscale shopping district worth the trek. Heritage buildings and cafes intermix with modern boutiques and high-end eateries. Massive murals add charm and open-air plazas invite rest stops after an afternoon spent on one of Vancouver's trendiest streets.

| START | END | LENGTH |
|---|---|---|
| Paul's Omelettery | Small Victory | 1.5km; one hour |

### 1 Begin With Breakfast

On the right side of Granville St, just past the southern end of the bridge, **Paul's Omelettery** (p105) is a breakfast legend. The menu is grounded in signature omelets, but also offers excellent eggs benedict and 'lumberjack breakfasts.' Dive into a heaping plate and then work it off as you speed-walk uphill to your next stop.

### 2 Pick Up A Gift

Head upstairs to large, under-the-radar **Pacific Arts Market** (p107) where creative artisan stands showcase the work of more than 40 Vancouver and BC artists. From paintings to jewelry, fiber arts to handmade chocolate bars, wares on offer make authentic souvenirs to take back home. Artists change regularly, and there's something for every budget.

### 3 Chocolate Stop

If you didn't find any chocolate at the market, drop by historic **Purdy's Chocolates** (p107), a homegrown confectionary chain with purple-hued shops found throughout the region. Cool off over an ice-cream bar or buy some treats for later.

### 4 Drinks & Dinner

You'll have spotted some enticing restaurants on your walk, covering cuisines from Japanese to Indian. But if you're starting to seriously mull your dinner options, check out the menu of Lebanese meze, wine and happy-hour specials at **Mazahr** (p106). Perch on the patio to people-watch over a platter of grilled meats and house-made dips.

### 5 Show Time

Just around the corner, handsome **Stanley Theatre** (p104) was built in 1930 and is one of the city's most popular performance venues. Check to see what's on. Consider booking tickets for an evening show.

### 6 Shopping Strip

This stretch of South Granville is lined on both sides with tempting boutiques, but well-curated **Bacci's** should be on everyone's shopping list. Check out its funky homewares and trendy fashions.

### 7 Snacks For Later

Not far from the area's posh Shaughnessy neighborhood, **Meinhardt Fine Foods** (p107) is a high-end Vancouver deli and grocery store. Explore the aisles of fancy goods and tempting treats, and pick up a pocket snack for later.

### 8 Coffee Break

Rest weary feet with a stop at **Small Victory** (p106), a quaint street-side cafe. Sip a coffee, snack on a sweet or savory freshly baked treat and – if you can snag one – people-watch from a seat by the window.

## EXPERIENCES

### Stroll Queen Elizabeth Park  PARK
MAP: ❶ P98 E7

At 125m above sea level, **Queen Elizabeth Park** is the city's highest point, offering panoramic views of the mountain-framed downtown skyscrapers. A tree-lover's dream, the 130-acre park claims to house specimens of every tree native to Canada. This is a good place to view local birdlife: keep your eyes peeled for chickadees, hummingbirds and huge bald eagles whirling overhead. This park is home to the domed Bloedel Conservatory and fine-dining restaurant **Seasons in the Park** (p105) at its top end. Picnics and pitch-and-putt are popular pastimes for locals here.

### Spot Tropical Birds at Bloedel  BIRDS
MAP: ❷ P98 E7

Housed at the highest point of picturesque Queen Elizabeth Park, **Bloedel Conservatory** *(vandusengarden.org; adult/child from $10/5)* is a delightful destination on a rainy day. Tropical trees and plants bristle with hundreds of free-flying, bright-plumaged birds. Listen for noisy resident parrots and keep your eyes peeled for rainbow-hued gouldian finches, shimmering African superb starlings and maybe even a dramatic lady amherst pheasant. Ask nicely and the attendants might allow you to feed smaller birds from a bowl. If the kids get antsy, ask for a free scavenger hunt sheet to track what they spot.

### Catch a Ballgame at the Stadium  SPORTS
MAP: ❸ P98 F7

Catching a Vancouver Canadians minor-league baseball game at old-school **Nat Bailey Stadium** *(www.milb.com/vancouver)*, known as 'the Nat' by locals, is a summer tradition for many Vancouverites. For some, the experience isn't complete unless you also add a hot dog, peanuts and some ice-cold beers to the ball game. Non-traditional options are available too, like sushi. Don't leave without checking out the Wall of Fame exhibit highlighting former Canadians players who have gone on to the majors.

### See a Show at Stanley Theatre  THEATER
MAP: ❹ P98 A2

Known as 'the Stanley' *(artsclub.com; tickets from $30)*, the art deco **Stanley Theatre** is part of the Arts Club Theatre Company, Vancouver's biggest. The heritage theater opened in the 1930s as a movie cinema and vaudeville house. It is now the flagship stage of Western Canada's largest theater company, showing everything from off-Broadway musicals to comedy shows and classic plays with up-and-coming actors. Unable to catch a show? The stunning exterior is worth a walk-by.

## LISTINGS

# Best Places for...

$ Budget   $$ Midrange   $$$ Top End

## Eating

### Upscale Dining

**Seasons in the Park** $$$

 E7

Take in panoramic views of the city and North Shore mountains from this upscale restaurant that sits at the top of Queen Elizabeth Park. Pair a glass of wine with dishes like wood-fired local salmon, Dungeness crab or stuffed mushrooms. *vancouverdine.com; 11:30am-8:30pm Sun-Thu, to 9pm Fri & Sat*

**Tojo's** $$$

6 C2

Credited as the first restaurant on Vancouver's now vibrant sushi scene, this upscale, internationally recognized restaurant is an experience. Chef Tojo's personalized omakase menu draws celebrity diners from around the world. *tojos.com; 5-9:30pm Mon-Sat*

**Gary's** $$$

 A2

Despite its casual feel, this upscale spot is Michelin-recognized, with French country-style cooking. Enjoy share-style small plates such as asparagus with saffron rouille or pork collar with parsley sauce. Prepare for surprises; the menu changes constantly. *garysrestaurant.ca; 5-10pm Tue-Sat*

**Vij's** $$$

8 E3

Lauded as the launch-point for Vancouver's Indian cuisine scene. It offers a one-page array of tempting dishes, but the trick is to order three or four to share (mains are available as small plates, and orders come with rice and naan). *vijs.ca; 5:30-10pm*

### Casual Eateries

**Paul's Omelettery** $

9 A1

This cozy, super-friendly place is superior to most bacon-and-eggs destinations. Omelets are its signature dish, but the eggs Benedict and heaping 'lumberjack breakfasts' are also excellent. Arrive early on weekends. *paulsomelettery.com; 7am-3pm*

**La Taqueria Pinche Taco Shop** $

10 E2

This wildly popular Mexican mini-chain combines communal tables, a large patio and inviting bar area with a full menu of favorites. Order a selection of tacos (al pastor and asada recommended) with beer from Vancouver-based South American brewery Andina. *lataqueria.com; 11:30am-9pm Mon-Wed, to 10pm Thu-Sat, to 8pm Sun*

**Salmon n' Bannock** $$

11 B2

Vancouver's only Indigenous restaurant serves fresh-made Indigenous-influenced dishes featuring local ingredients. The juicy salmon 'n' bannock burger has been a staple for years. More elaborate, feast-like options include game sausages and bison

**See p98** for map of locations

EXPLORE

FAIRVIEW & SOUTH GRANVILLE

105

Tojo's (p105)

pot roast. *salmonandbannock.net; 3-9pm Mon-Sat, 10am-2pm & 3-9pm Sun*

### Mazahr Lebanese Kitchen $$
**12** A2

Opened by former partner of Jamjar restaurant, Mazahr provides the city with a taste of Lebanon, offering dishes that remind the chef of home. *mazahr.ca; noon-8:30pm Tue-Thu, to 9pm Fri & Sat*

# Drinking

## Beer & Cocktails

### Grapes & Soda
**13** A1

This warm, small-table hangout self-identifies as a 'natural wine bar,' with well-curated options from BC, Europe and beyond. It also serves excellent cocktails: from the countless bottles behind the bar, the staff can seemingly concoct anything you desire. *grapesandsoda.ca; 5-11pm Mon-Sat*

### Bar Asra
**14** A2

A great addition to the Granville St strip (around the corner on 11th), this new spot serves creative cocktails and tasty share plates in a chic space filled with lush greenery and wood decor. *bar-asra.com; 3-10pm Tue-Wed, to 11pm Thu-Sat*

### Caffé Barney
**15** A3

Known as the 'Barnyard' by locals, this upbeat cafe is a bustling brunch spot (lunch and dinner available too) with a full bar. Choose a pint of local craft beer from the dozens on tap, or go for a cocktail. *caffebarney.com; hours vary*

## Coffee Shops

### Small Victory
**16** A3

The South Granville branch of this local chain serves up a sophisticated coffee program. If you can find one, snag a seat at the swanky white-and-gold bar and sip a silky-smooth latte. Feeling snacky? Add a flaky butter croissant to your order. *smallvictory.ca; 8am-5pm*

### Beaucoup
**17** A1

This French-approach bakeshop arguably serves the best croissants and pains au chocolat in the city. Add coffee and a bite-sized kouign-amann pastry perhaps, then tackle the lovely Arbutus Greenway walking route that starts across the street. *beaucoupbakery.com; 8am-5pm*

### Aperture Coffee Bar
**18** F2

This neighborhood coffee shop is ideal for hanging out on a rainy day, especially if you dip into its shelves of loaner books. The coffee is good here, and light meals like wraps and sandwiches are available. *aperturecoffeebar.com; 8am-10pm*

### Dose Espresso Bar
**19** A2

From perfectly executed espressos to rich nutella mochas, this blink-and-you'll-miss-it hole-in-the-wall is committed to making excellent java. *facebook.com/doseespressobar; 7:30am-2:30pm Mon-Fri, 9am-noon Sat*

# Shopping

## Gifts & Homewares

### Pacific Arts Market
**20** A2

Shop for original art prints and handmade gifts in one of Vancouver's best art spaces. Check the website for monthly free-entry social gatherings with live music and artist meet-and-greets – a great way to connect with the local art scene. *pacificartsmarket.ca; hours vary*

### Book Warehouse
**21** D2

Locals routinely beeline to this browse-worthy bookstore for discounts on new and just-released titles. If you're not sure what you're looking for, ask the great staff for recommendations. *book warehouse.ca; 10am-6pm*

### Ian Tan Art Gallery
**22** A1

This popular stop on the city's gallery row focuses on contemporary Canadian artists. You'll find lots of bold, often bright, paintings and installations on the walls here, and it's a great place to put your finger on the pulse of Canada's modern art scene. Buy everything, from small prints to large-scale original paintings. *iantangallery.com; 11am-5pm Tue-Sat, from noon Sun*

### Walrus
 E4

Small but brilliantly curated, with must-have accessories and homewares, mostly from Canadian designers. Form meets function here, so give yourself plenty of time to browse pottery knickknacks and quirky artisan jewelry. *walrushome.com; hours vary*

### Bacci's
**24** A2

Combining designer women's clothing with perfectly curated trinkets, Bacci's is a dangerous place to browse. Before you know it, you'll have an armful of chunky luxury soaps, embroidered cushions and picture-perfect coffee mugs to fit in your suitcase. *baccisvancouver.com; 9:45am-5:30pm Mon-Sat*

## Snacks & Sweets

### Purdy's Chocolates
 A2

This purple-painted chocolatier is a homegrown BC business, with outlets dotted across the city. Go for chocolate hedgehogs, orange melty bars or sweet Georgia browns (pecans in caramel and chocolate). *purdys.com; 9:30am-5:30pm Mon-Sat*

### Meinhardt Fine Foods
**26** A3

Narrow aisles at this swanky deli and grocery spot are lined with international condiments, luxury canned goods and treats that everyone should try at least once. Build a perfect picnic from tempting bread, cheese and cold cuts, or snag a house-made deli sandwich. *meinhardtfinefoods.com; 8am-9pm Mon-Sat, to 8pm Sun*

**See p120** for eating, drinking and shopping listings

# Explore
# Kitsilano & UBC

Vancouver's West Side is home to two of the city's most distinctive neighborhoods: Kitsilano and the University of British Columbia (UBC). Kitsilano or 'Kits' blends laid-back beach vibes with heritage charm in its sandy beaches, historic homes and lively shopping and dining stretching along the popular West 4th Avenue. Beyond Kits, the UBC campus wraps around the peninsula's western tip, where you'll find tree-lined trails, public gardens and a great mix of museums and cultural attractions. Balance a day visiting these neighborhoods with boutique browsing, museum hopping and sunbathing by the sea – an inviting detour from downtown.

## Getting Around

 **Bus**
Buses run frequently and offer quick access to both neighborhoods. Kitsilano and UBC are well-connected by bus, with routes like the 99 B-Line and 4 linking downtown to West 4th Avenue, Broadway and UBC's main campus.

 **Bike**
The area is ideal for cycling, with designated bike routes along scenic paths connecting parks, beaches, Kitsilano and UBC.

 **On Foot**
Exploring Kitsilano and UBC is easily walkable. Start in Kitsilano, where quiet rural streets connect to lively commercial strips like West 4th and Broadway, both full of shops and eateries.

### THE BEST

**LIVELY BEACH** Kitsilano Beach (p118)

**CULTURAL MUSEUM** Museum of Anthropology (p112)

**TRANQUIL GARDEN** Nitobe Memorial Garden (p115)

**SHOPPING STRIP** West 4th Ave (p118)

**OUTDOOR POOL** Kitsilano Pool (p117)

Kitsilano Beach (p118)
IRRA/SHUTTERSTOCK

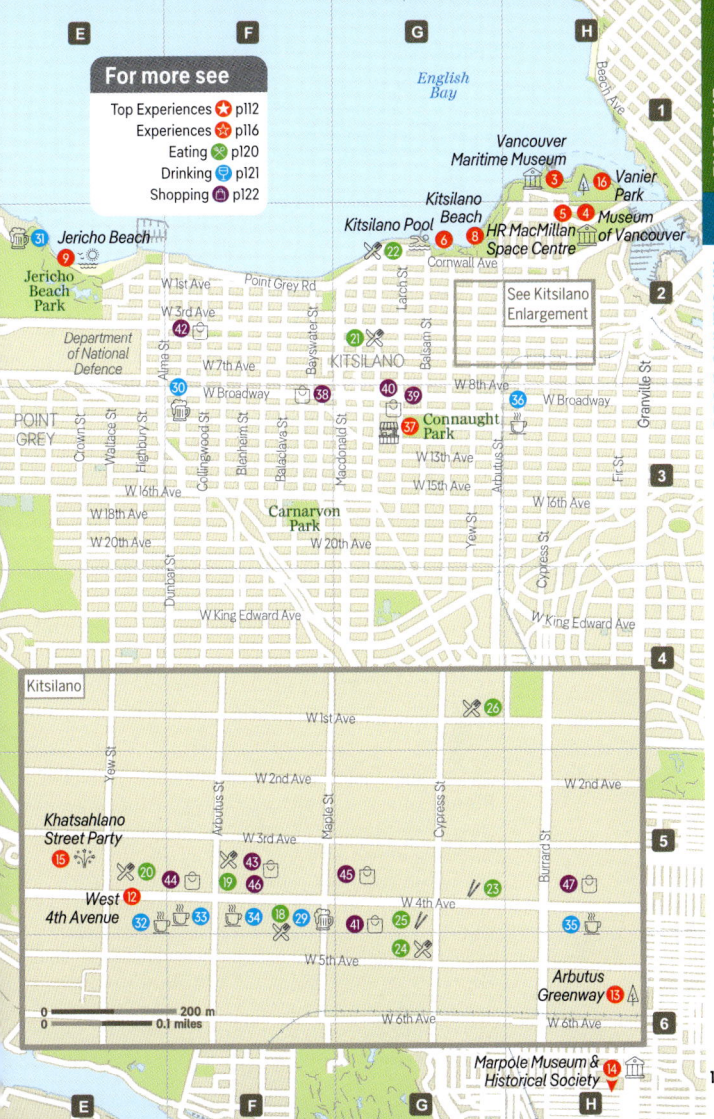

⭐ **TOP EXPERIENCE**

# Museum of Anthropology

Vancouver's best museum, **MOA** *(moa.ubc.ca; adult/child $26/13)*, is the UBC campus' main draw. The museum is home to one of Canada's finest and most important collections of Northwest Coast aboriginal art and artifacts. But that's just the start: moving beyond local treasures, the ambitious collection illuminates global cultures too.

MAP P110 **C4**

**PLANNING TIP**
Give yourself at least a couple of hours to explore; it's easy to immerse yourself here. On a budget? Entry on Thursday evening after 5pm costs $10.

Scan this QR code for the latest list of exhibits.

### Great Hall
The standout feature of this Arthur Erickson–designed museum is the Great Hall, a grand space filled with a forest of towering totem poles and carved ceremonial figures, house posts and historic exhibits. Many of the ornate carvings are vibrantly colored: look for smiling masks and a life-sized row boat containing two figures ready to head out to sea. Massive floor-to-ceiling windows offer stunning views of the nearby waterfront and mountains, creating a dramatic backdrop for the wide open space. The Hall is the main entrance for the museum and also the starting point for free guided tours offered several times a day.

### Immersive Galleries
The jam-packed **Multiversity Galleries** showcase more than 10,000 fascinating ethnographic artifacts from cultures around the world. Closely packed into display cabinets, they're a sensory immersion: find everything from Kenyan snuff bottles and Maori stone knives to ancient Greek jugs and Swedish lace doilies. A visit to MOA isn't complete without seeing the **Bill Reid Rotunda**, displaying the Haida artist's famous sculpture *The Raven and the First Men*. Then pop into the **European Ceramics Gallery**. Sometimes overlooked

PHOTO BY MICHAEL ELKAN, COURTESY OF THE MUSEUM OF ANTHROPOLOGY AT UBC, VANCOUVER, CANADA

by visitors clambering to see the totem poles, it's a subtle stunner, created from a private collection of hundreds of pieces of delicately beautiful pottery and porcelain crafted between the 16th and 19th centuries.

## Outdoor Exhibits

For those visiting on a sunny day, the museum grounds offer a chance to explore more. Two **Haida Houses** constructed by Bill Reid and Namgis artist Doug Cranmer are here, alongside the **Yosef Wosk Reflecting Pond**, a tranquil spot where you can sit by the water and soak up mountain views. Around the pond, memorial poles from 1951 to present day reach for the sky. A short walking trail allows you to stretch your legs.

**QUICK BREAK**
The MOA is a short walk from **Koerner's Pub**, where you can drink and dine with students. Time your visit well and you can also pick up treats from the UBC Farm Markets.

# WALKING TOUR

# Walk UBC Campus & Gardens

The region's biggest university campus has ample attractions for a full day out. Transit makes UBC easy to reach from downtown. This walk takes you to some of UBC's best and also lesser-known attractions. Keep your eyes peeled for public artworks dotting the campus.

| START | END | LENGTH |
|---|---|---|
| Morris & Helen Belkin Art Gallery | UBC Botanical Garden | 3km; 1½ hours |

### ❶ Contemporary Art Stop

One of Vancouver's oldest contemporary art spaces, the **Morris & Helen Belkin Art Gallery** showcases thought-provoking contemporary art exploring social, political and cultural themes. With a strong focus on research, underrepresented voices and critical dialogue, the gallery also offers talks, tours and public programs –all free and open to the public.

### ❷ Hidden Garden

The campus is studded with landscaped gardens and green spaces, but the one outside the **UBC Asian Centre** is arguably the most hidden and unusual. It's a great spot for quiet contemplation away from the campus crowds. Check out the hulking rock garden boulders here, each inscribed with Confucian philosophies.

### ❸ Japanese Botanicals

The tranquil **Nitobe Memorial Garden** *(adult/child $7/4)* is a traditional Japanese garden honoring Dr Inazō Nitobe whose lifelong goal was to connect cultures. Walk peaceful pathways, across small bridges and around a pond filled with plump koi. Spot turtles basking in the sun, admire springtime cherry blossoms, and stop at the teahouse. Watch for summertime guided tours.

### ❹ Behold Big Blue

Discover the variety of flora and fauna in the area and beyond at Vancouver's **Beaty Biodiversity Museum** *(beatymuseum.ubc.ca; adult/child $18/10)*. Take in the blue-whale skeleton on display: this is one of the few places in the world you can get an up-close look at the remains of the largest creature to ever exist on Earth.

### ❺ Bare Beach

If you're feeling adventurous, look for the signs for Trail 6, walk between the trees and descend the 490 wooden steps down to **Wreck Beach** (p118). Vancouver's official naturist beach (clothing is optional) provides the perfect opportunity to drop your drawers with like-minded locals.

### ❻ Botanical Garden

Make sure you put your pants back on before reaching the final attraction. **UBC Botanical Garden** (p116) is a verdant green space, divided into dense forest on one side and several themed horticultural areas on the other.

### ❼ Treetop Views

If you're visiting from April to October, before leaving the UBC Botanical Garden, be sure to take a stroll along the **Greenheart TreeWalk** (p116). The aerial trail system takes you from tree to tree through coastal temperate rainforest and provides a squirrel's-eye view of the forest floor below.

## EXPERIENCES

### Bask in Blooms at UBC Botanical Garden  GARDEN

Enjoy a huge array of rhododendrons, a fascinating apothecary plot, and a winter-green space of cold-weather bloomers at the **UBC Botanical Garden** (MAP: ❶ P110 D6; *botanicalgarden.ubc.ca; adult/child $11/5).* But this 28-hectare complex of themed gardens is home to more than just flowers. Before you leave, be sure to get a bird's eye view of the forest floor below with a stroll along the seasonal **Greenheart TreeWalk** (MAP: ❷ P110 D6; *adult/child $25/11),* open April to October. The elevated canopy walkway hangs from huge Douglas firs about 25m above the ground, taking you from tree to tree through a coastal temperate rainforest. It's family-friendly, but children aged 12 and under must must be accompanied by an adult. To take in both garden and tree walk, buy a combined ticket covering both (adult/child $28/13).

### See Ships at Vancouver Maritime Museum  MUSEUM
MAP: ❸ P110 H1

Packed with maritime charm, the waterfront **Vancouver Maritime Museum** *(vanmaritime.com; adult/child $22/17)* offers a fascinating glimpse into nautical history. Inside the distinctive A-frame building, you'll find an impressive collection of maritime artifacts, a variety of detailed ship models, and sections of boats that have been carefully reconstructed for an immersive walk-through experience. The museum highlight is the *Saint Roch,* a historic Arctic patrol vessel from 1928, once operated by the Royal Canadian Mounted Police. This was the first ship to complete a journey through the Northwest Passage in both directions. Museum admission includes scheduled access to tour this iconic vessel – you can even test your skills at steering it using an engaging wheelhouse simulator.

### Make Your Way to MOV  MUSEUM
MAP: ❹ P110 H2

Canada's largest civic museum, the **Museum of Vancouver** *(MOV; museumofvancouver.ca; adult/youth $23/18),* connects Vancouver to the world while showcasing the city's unique identity, both past and present. Out front, an iconic steel crab sculpture by George Norris has stood in front of the museum since 1968 as a symbol of the First Nations legend of the crab as protector of the harbour.

Inside, permanent galleries showcase everything from First Nations artifacts and pioneer-era items to eye-catching neon signs and 1960s counterculture displays capturing Kitsilano's flower-power past. More recent exhibits spotlight local design, social history and efforts toward cultural repair, and offer fresh perspectives on the city's evolving identity. Interactive features such as vintage music stations and recreated historical settings bring the past to life, while thoughtful temporary shows keep the content current and relevant. The museum shop complements the experience with locally inspired books, art and gifts.

## See the Stars at HR MacMillan Space Centre    SPACE CENTER

MAP: ❺ P110 **H2**

Just steps from the MOV, in Vanier Park, the **HR MacMillan Space Centre** *(spacecentre.ca; adult/child $24/21)* is a favorite among star-gazing kids. Focused on the wonderful world of space, the astronomy museum includes a gallery of hands-on exhibits (don't miss the Mars section, where you can drive across the surface in a simulator) as well as live science demonstrations and a cool 45-minute show in the upstairs Planetarium Star Theatre. Check the daily schedule of events, presentations and shows online before you arrive. Saturday-night planetarium performances are popular with locals and typically draw a more adult crowd.

## Cool Off At Kitsilano Pool    POOL

MAP: ❻ P110 **G2**

North America's longest outdoor swimming pool can be found at the water's edge on Vancouver's most vibrant beach, Kitsilano Beach (p118) or Kits Beach. Perched on the ocean, the heated salt-water **Kitsilano Pool** *(adult/child $7/5)* – open mid-May to mid-September, and known as Kits Pool locally – is one of the city's most popular places to play on a warm summer day. The recently renovated swimming pool has a designated kids' area with a gradual entry popular with families and children learning to swim, plus lanes to practice your laps. The first pool opened here in 1931, and was replaced in 1978. A new pool is being discussed as part of Vancouver's 2027–2030 Capital Plan, so be sure to take a dip before then.

## Visit Morris & Helen Balkin Art Gallery    GALLERY

MAP: ❼ P110 **C4**

Formerly called the UBC Fine Arts Gallery and the only space where Vancouverites could view contemporary art at the time, the **Morris & Helen Belkin Art Gallery** has since become an ever-intriguing gallery that specializes in contemporary art. Its collection contains more than 5000 artworks, making it one of the province's largest public art collections. Through research-based exhibitions, publications and academic collaborations, the gallery engages deeply with contemporary issues in art history, criticism and curation. Check ahead for workshops and presentations, often covering key or emerging themes in avant-garde art.

## BEST BEACHES

### Kitsilano Beach
MAP: **8** P110 **G2**
The city's best all-around beach, balancing sporty action (beach volleyball and basketball are big) and chilling on the sand.

### Jericho Beach
MAP: **9** P110 **E2**
Prime skyline and sunset views. Stand-up paddle board and kayak rentals. Each third weekend in July, the beach stages Vancouver's popular Folk Music Festival.

### Spanish Banks Beach
MAP: **10** P110 **C1**
Beach party central, with grassy areas, picnic tables, beach volleyball courts and the city's largest off-leash dog park.

### Wreck Beach
MAP: **11** P110 **B5**
Clothing is optional and drum circles are constant on North America's biggest nude beach. Access the sand by by a long, steep stairway.

### Shop West 4th Ave  SHOPPING
MAP: **12** P110 **E5**
For some of the city's best boutiques and street-side patios, head to **West 4th Avenue** just blocks from Kitsilano Beach. From yoga pants (the Lululemon here was the first standalone location) to chic modern footwear, you can shop for some of the city's top fashion finds. Grab a bite to eat – Sophie's Cosmic Cafe (p120) is a local fave for brunch – or a snack from one of the many ice-cream shops, sushi joints and cafes lining the eight-block stretch of shops. Admire upscale, tree-lined residential streets along the way.

### Walk the Arbutus Greenway  PARK
A cool linear park, **Arbutus Greenway** (MAP: **13** P110 **H6**) is a 9km-long walking and cycling route along a disused urban rail line that's been transformed by the city. Running south to Fraser River, the greenway is a popular and accessible nature-hugging pathway where you can expect to spot birdlife, butterflies and lots of wildflowers. There are bike-share stations en route, should you choose to cycle.

You don't have to walk the whole thing – popular stops include the shops and restaurants of Kerrisdale (just east of Kits), and the **Marpole Museum & Historical Society** (MAP: **14** P110 **H6**; *marpolehistorical.ca*) a historic house furnished as a working-class residence from the early 1900s. Inside tours must be booked ahead. Check the website for special events available to the public.

**Khatsahlano Street Party**

### Catch Khatsahlano — FESTIVAL

If you're in town in July, add Vancouver's largest free music and arts festival to your calendar. A 10-block stretch of the bustling West 4th area sets the stage for top local performers and artisans, plus great food and a beer garden, during the **Khatsahlano Street Party** (MAP: 15 P110 **E5**; *khatsahlano.ca*). Kitsilano's largest and most popular annual event, it honors its original founder with live music, food and local vendors.

Kitsilano takes its name from Chief Khatsahlano, whose First Nations village, Sun'ahk, once stood where **Vanier Park** (MAP: 16 P110 **H1**) is today. In 1901, the community was forcibly displaced, with families relocated to reserves in Capilano and Squamish. Kits grew rapidly after a streetcar line arrived in 1905, leading to a housing boom. By the 1960s, many homes housed UBC students, and the area became known as a 'beatnik ghetto' and hub for counterculture. One group of antinuclear activists would go on to form what we now know as Greenpeace.

# LISTINGS

# Best Places for...

**$** Budget  **$$** Midrange  **$$$** Top End

See p110 for map of locations

## Eating

### Breakfast & Brunch

**Jamjar Canteen $**
 D5

Dining at this smaller branch of the highly popular Lebanese comfort-food restaurant chain means choosing a main (lamb sausages or deep-fried cauliflower recommended), then adding a base: rice bowl, salad bowl or wrap. Top with olives, veggies, hummus, etc. *jamjarcanteen.ca; 10:30am-10pm Mon-Fri, from 11am Sat & Sun*

**Their There $**
 F5

This trendy cafe is known for its house-made mochi donuts, gooey breakfast sandwiches and great coffee. Dive into a gourmet sandwich (pork cubano!) or an array of inventive goodies, often including caramel popcorn cronuts, and kimchi- and pork-belly stuffed croissants. *theirthere.ca; 9am-4pm Tue-Sun*

**Sophie's Cosmic Cafe $$**
 F5

Vancouver's best retro diner, where breakfast is the best reason to snag a booth. Try the bulging Spanish omelet. Expect long lines on weekends. *sophiescosmiccafe.com; 8am-3pm*

**Jam Cafe Kitsilano $$**
 E5

The line at this Southern comfort food address is worth the wait. Consider ordering the fried chicken benny or a giant breakfast bowl. *jamcafes.com; 8am-2:30pm Mon-Fri, to 3pm Sat & Sun*

### Casual Eateries

**Naam $**
 G2

A relic of Kitsilano's hippie past, this vegetarian spot feels like a comfy farmhouse. Peak times are packed, but it's worth the wait for the hearty stir fries, curry specials and ever-popular fries with miso gravy. *thenaam.com; 11am-11pm Mon-Fri, from 9am Sat & Sun*

**SImpatico Ristorante $**
 G2

Serving Greco-Roman cuisine combining Anatolian, Cyprian and mainland Greek flavors, this family-owned address is a great spot to stop for roast lamb or souvlaki while shopping on West 4th. The pizza is delicious too. *simpaticorestaurant.ca; 4:30-9:30pm Sun-Thu, to 10pm Fri & Sat*

**Ramen Danbo $**
 G5

Behind a black-wood exterior and oversized paper lantern lurks the chatty heart of Kitsilano's best ramen joint. The cozy, izakaya-like spot serves its slurp-worthy bowls in four base variations. *ramendanbo.com; 11am-11pm*

### Fine Dining

**Fable Kitchen $$**
 G6

One of Vancouver's favorite farm-to-table

restaurants is a lovely rustic-chic room of exposed brick, wood beams and prominently displayed red rooster logos. Expect perfectly prepared bistro dishes showcasing local seasonal ingredients such as duck, pork and scallops. Brunch available. *fable kitchen.ca; 11am-2pm & 5pm-9pm, 9am-2pm Sat & Sun*

### Maenam 👁👁

 G5

Kitsilano's best modern Thai restaurant reinvents traditional Thai menus. Start with the familiar (even the pad Thai is different), but try something new too: the lamb shank with red cumin curry is delicious. *maenam.ca; 5-10pm Sun-Tue, noon-2pm & 5-10pm Wed-Sat*

### AnnaLena 👁👁👁

26 G4

An elegant-but-casual resto-bar with some serious foodie chops, this elongated lounge-like room (think monochrome decor and brushed concrete floors) is the setting for superbly prepared dishes, from bison tartare to succulent grilled octopus to house-made ice-cream. *annalena.ca; 5-9pm*

### Wildlight Kitchen + Bar 👁👁👁

 B2

This light-filled restaurant near UBC's Lelәm̓ Village serves fresh seafood-forward dishes like seared hokkaido scallops and golden eagle sablefish. Its executive chef, Warren Chow, is the recipient of the 2023 Michelin Young Chef Award. *wildlightrestaurant.ca; 11am-10pm*

## Drinking

### Casual Pubs

### Koerner's Pub

 C4

UBC's best pub welcomes with communal tables, a foliage-fringed patio and an excellent drink list. Dive into a BC craft beer and organic burger. The crunchy UBC farm harvest salad, largely sourced from the on-campus farm, is recommended. *koerners. ca; noon-11pm Tue-Fri, to 8pm Mon*

### Bimini's Public House

 F5

A city staple since 1975, this is a great local pub for meeting new friends and catching a game.

There's a good array of craft beers, including BC favorites Phillips and Parallel 49. Check out the table football and arcade games near the entrance. *biminispub.ca; 8am-1am Mon-Thu, to 2am Fri & Sat, to 10:30pm Sun*

### Wolf & Hound

 F3

Sidewalk seating and live music draw locals to this friendly neighborhood pub, named after the band of Irish musician-turned-Vancouverite Danny Burns. Swig an ice cold pint of Guinness and nosh delicious pub grub. *wolfandhound.ca; hours vary*

### Galley Patio & Grill

31 E2

At sunset, plop down on a plastic patio chair and order a tasty local beer like a red devil pale ale from R&B Brewing. Pub grub includes salmon burgers and beer-battered fish and chips. *thegalley.ca; 11:30am-8pm Tue-Fri, from 11am Sat-Mon*

### Coffee & Tea

### 49th Parallel Coffee

 E5

Sit with locals in the glass-enclosed, conservatory-like area at Kitsilano's favorite coffee-shop hangout and sip a latte from a turquoise cup. Be sure to sample as many Lucky's Doughnuts as you can. Need a recommendation? Try an apple-bacon fritter. *49thcoffee.com; 7am-6pm Mon-Thu, to 7pm Fri-Sun*

### O5 Teas Rare Tea Bar
 **F5**

This tea-lover's haven is the place to slow down and explore the rich wonders of the leaf. Perch on a stool at the counter or snag the wooden table by the window and prepare for a tea-based voyage of discovery. *O5tea.com; noon-6pm Mon-Thu, to 8pm Fri & Sat, to 7pm Sun*

### Silk Road Tea
 **F5**

This satellite branch of Victoria's favorite fancy-tea emporium combines friendly staff with hundreds of lip-smacking leafy varieties. A bag of Berry Victoria is a recommended souvenir, while the fragrant Angelwater has a cult local following. *silkroadteastore.com; 11am-5:30pm Wed-Sat, to 4:30pm Sun*

### Elysian Coffee
 **H5**

A smaller, cozier location of the mini Vancouver chain, Elysian Kits offers quality coffee in a welcoming atmosphere. Espresso-based drinks, single-origin coffees and carefully curated blends are all roasted in-house. *elysiancoffee.com; 7am-6pm Mon-Fri, 8am-6pm Sat, to 4pm Sun*

### Pallet Coffee Roasters
 **H3**

Pallet roasts its own coffee and serves a standout open-face spicy chicken melt. Otherwise, the spacious cafe features ample seating, a striking communal table, and a beautiful bar for espresso drinks and pour-overs. *palletcoffeeroasters.com; 8am-3pm*

# Shopping

## Snacks & Sweets

### Kitsilano Farmers Market
**37** **G3**

This seasonal farmers' market is one of the city's most popular. Arrive early for the best selection – you'll have the pick of freshly plucked local fruit and veg, such as sweet strawberries or spectacularly flavorful heirloom tomatoes. *eatlocal.org; 8am-2pm Sun May-Oct*

### Koko Monk
**38** **F3**

A little chocolate-shop-and-cafe combo, Koko specializes in raw chocolate with sophisticated and complex flavors. Try the pastries and lip-smacking hot chocolate menu, and buy chocolate bars for sweet-toothed friends back home. *kokomonk.com; noon-8pm*

### Thomas Haas
**39** **G3**

The small tables at this independent chocolatier are often filled with customers sipping coffee and nibbling decadent pastries. But there's also a retail counter where regulars buy house-made chocolate bars and bonbon boxes. *thomashaas.com; 8am-5:30pm Mon-Sat*

## Books & Records

### Kidsbooks
**40** **G3**

Canada's biggest children's bookshop has thousands of novels, picture books and anything else you can think of to keep bookworms happy. There are regular author events, plus quality toys and games. *kidsbooks.ca; 10am-5:30pm Mon-Sat, from 11am Sun*

### Zulu Records
**41** G5

It's easy to blow an afternoon flipping through the vinyl and CD selection at Kitsilano's favorite indie music store. It also sells local show tickets, and knowledgeable staff can point you to essential Vancouver recordings worth buying. *facebook.com/zulurecords.store; hours vary*

### Banyen Books & Sound
**42** F2

A Kitsilano staple since 1970, Banyen sells metaphysical books, crystals, yoga and meditation supplies, plus incense and tarot cards. This is the spot to buy unique gifts for spiritual seekers, wellness explorers and curious minds. *banyen.com; 11am-7pm*

## Fashion Finds
### Melanie Auld
**43** F5

The Vancouver flagship of sought-after Canadian jewelry brand Melanie Auld has beautiful displays of demi-fine jewelry, a welded-bracelet station and a piercing room. *melanieauld.com; 11am-6pm*

### Poppy Barley
**44** F5

A Certified B Corporation, Poppy Barley creates luxury footwear (boots, flats and heels), handbags and backpacks for women at a fair price. Co-owned by sisters, the brand rethinks every step of how it creates its sustainable products, designed to be worn on repeat. *poppybarley.com; 10am-6pm*

### Old Faithful
**45** G5

Inspired by owner Walter Manning's grandparents' shop, this modern-day version of a general provisions store features quality products with beautiful design elements. It aspires to sell trusty, well-built heirloom pieces – furniture, lighting, books, bags et al – that are only enhanced by the passage of time. *oldfaithfulshop.com; 11am-6pm*

## Sports & Outdoors
### Arc'teryx
**46** F5

Flagship branch of Vancouver's high-end outdoor-gear store. Expect to pay a premium for the finest waterproof jackets and weather-resistant pants. The upside is: they'll last for ages and you'll be joining a cool group of outdoorsy types wearing a highly regarded logo. *arcteryx.com; 10am-7pm Mon-Sat, 11am-6pm Sun*

### Pacific Boarder
**47** H5

A spacious and energetic shop offering a diverse selection of high-quality snowboarding, skateboarding and surfing gear, along with stylish apparel for outdoor and action sports enthusiasts. *pacificboarder.com; 10am-6pm Mon-Thu, to 8pm Fri, to 5pm Sun*

## ★ WORTH A TRIP

# Richmond

When you arrive at Vancouver International Airport (YVR), you're technically in Richmond, Vancouver's sister suburb. Before heading into Vancouver, spend a few days here. Richmond boasts amazing Asian cuisine, the largest night market in North America and a charming fishing village – especially enjoyable mid-May to June during spot prawn season.

**PLANNING TIP**
If you're heading to Victoria, Nanaimo or the Gulf Islands, skip downtown Vancouver. Harbour Air's direct floatplane service from the airport's south terminal is ideal for day trips and avoiding highway traffic.

Scan this QR code for sample Richmond itineraries.

### Getting There
If you don't visit immediately upon arrival by plane, Richmond is about 20 minutes by car or 30 to 45 minutes by bus from Vancouver. The Canada Line SkyTrain also connects Richmond to downtown Vancouver and Vancouver International Airport, with several stops around Richmond.

### Richmond Night Market
Often compared to the night markets in Hong Kong or Singapore, ❶ **Richmond Night Market** (pictured p126; *richmondnightmarket.com; adult/child $7/free*) takes it to the next level with over 500 items to taste at 100-plus food stalls. The largest of its kind in North America, the night market showcases the city's culinary scene, highlighting the best eats, bites and bevvies from other global destinations, including Indonesia, Turkey, Mexico and Barbados. From Japanese poutine to churros and butter beer, you can eat here for hours, working it off in between with a stroll through vendor stalls. There are always new offerings: check the list of the month's 10 most popular vendors displayed at the entrance.

The food may be the biggest draw, but there's much more to do here. A stage for live performances raises the curtain on nightly entertainment – musical acts, martial arts displays, dance showcases and more. Kids can jump the night away on a bouncy castle. A games area, candy-colored forest and oversized prop chairs also lure little ones.

## Steveston Village

Sitting where the Fraser River meets the Salish Sea, Steveston Village is a working fishing harbor with quaint small-town vibes. ❷**Fisherman's Wharf** is the main hub, with harbor views and a variety of local shops and restaurants. From Fisherman's Wharf, head on foot towards ❸**Garry Point Park** along **Fishers Walk**, a free outdoor trail showcasing Steveston's vibrant fishing industry through bold visuals and fun facts about local marine life and culture. When spot prawn

**QUICK BREAK**
Sample the best fish n' chips at floating eatery ❹**Pajo's** or old-school strip spot ❺**Dave's Fish & Chips**. Which is better is hotly debated.

**SKY VIEW**
Richmond Night Market is home to the world's first and only night-market zipline ($25), providing a thrilling way to get a bird's eye view of the market excitement below.

season arrives (mid-May to June), the docks buzz with activity. This is the best time to sample the freshest seafood, often sold to locals and chefs straight from the boats.

Fish is a focus here, but the compact village offers more than superb seafood. Surrounded by fertile farmland producing everything from blueberries to bok choy, Steveston is a place where the farm-to-table approach is a way of life. The local dining scene reflects this: menus are packed with fresh seafood and produce. Add in scenic boardwalks, colorful fishing boats bobbing in the harbor and the historic ❻**Moncton Street** strip that once stood in for coastal New England on screen, and you've got the makings of a perfect seaside escape.

**Richmond Night Market (p124)**

## Dumpling Trail

Richmond's food scene is packed with regional Asian dishes, some rarely found outside of the Pacific. Get a taste of the city's top spots with a self-guided tasting tour along the **Dumpling Trail** *(dumplingtrail.ca),* a carefully curated route of 20 eateries serving up everything from steaming wonton soup dumplings to crispy fried pork pouches. Though not a literal trail of dumplings, the tasty journey leads food lovers to some of the best dumpling spots around town, including hidden stalls you would otherwise not notice. Be sure to do dim sum – the quintessential Chinese brunch is the best way to consume Cantonese cuisine, where a variety of dumplings are served in small portions and enjoyed family-style, traditionally paired with hot jasmine tea.

## Gulf of Georgia Cannery

Take a step back in time with a visit to the ❼ **Gulf of Georgia Cannery** *(gulfofgeorgiacannery.org),* one of BC's most compelling heritage attractions. Perched on wooden pilings above Fraser River, this well-preserved 19th-century salmon cannery offers a vivid look into the once-booming West Coast fishing industry. Designated a national historic site, it commemorates the rise of Canada's fishing economy from the 1870s to today. Recommended volunteer-led tours (free) bring the cannery's stories to life with detail and historical insight.

**WHERE CHEFS SHOP**

**Nutcha Phanthoupheng**, *executive chef and co-owner of Baan Lao Fine Thai Cuisine, sources directly from farmers and fishers.*

Many chefs buy fresh seafood – rockfish, spot prawns and salmon – directly from the boats at **Fisherman's Wharf** floating fish market. Family-owned ❽ **Richmond Country Farms Market** has great produce alongside donkeys, llamas and goats.

**See p138** for eating, drinking and shopping listings

# Explore
# North Shore

Framed by massive mountains, Vancouver's North Shore is your gateway to three major ski and snowboard areas. Save time to explore the south foot of North Vancouver, a scenic waterfront area comprising the action-packed Shipyards District and Lonsdale Quay (a public market). Then stroll up steep Lonsdale Ave for its row of tasty restaurants and varied local shops; the area also has its own buzzing brewery district. Next, head either east to Deep Cove for small village vibes and fun on the water, or further north to check out one of the city's top tourist sites, the Capilano Suspension Bridge.

## Getting Around

 **SeaBus**
A 15-minute SeaBus ride from downtown Vancouver brings you to North Van's Shipyards District.

 **Bus**
City buses connect Lower Lonsdale to the nearby mountains. Free summer shuttles from downtown run to Grouse Mountain and Capilano Suspension Bridge.

 **StreetCart**
June to September, the free, electric Lonsdale StreetCart departs from Polygon Gallery, stopping at shops and attractions.

 **Bike**
Rent wheels in Lower Lonsdale or at Lonsdale Quay to explore the waterfront and nearby trails. For a one-way ride, try public-shared Lime e-bikes.

**Capilano Suspension Bridge (p132)**
MINGANE/SHUTTERSTOCK

### THE BEST

**ALPINE ADVENTURES**
Grouse Mountain (p133)

**OUTDOOR ATTRACTION**
Capilano Suspension Bridge (p132)

**SHOPPING SPOT** Lower Lonsdale (p134)

**SCENIC HIKE** Quarry Rock (p136)

**ANIMAL ENCOUNTER**
Maplewood Farm (p137)

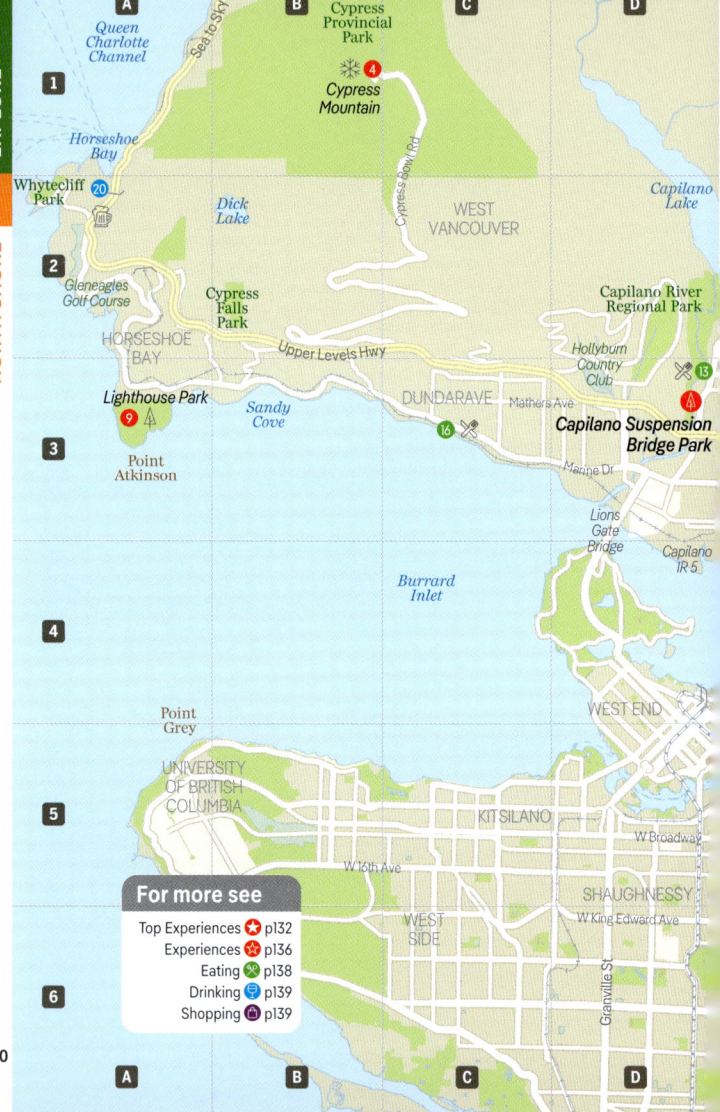

**For more see**
- Top Experiences ⭐ p132
- Experiences ✴ p136
- Eating ✖ p138
- Drinking 🅱 p139
- Shopping 🛍 p139

# NORTH SHORE

## Map Locations

- Grouse Mountain
- Lynn Headwaters Regional Park
- Mt Seymour Provincial Recreation Area
- Grouse Grind
- Mosquito Creek Park
- Vancouver Harbour
- Mt Seymour Provincial Park
- North Vancouver
- Lynn Canyon Ecology Centre
- Lynn Canyon Park
- Quarry Rock
- Deep Cove
- Honey Doughnuts & Goodies
- Indian Arm
- Maplewood Farm
- Cates Park
- Second Narrows Bridge
- Renfrew
- Renfrew Heights
- Burnaby
- Knight Road
- South Main

131

## ★ TOP EXPERIENCE

# Capilano Suspension Bridge

Swaying gently above the Capilano Canyon 70m below, the **Capilano Suspension Bridge** *(adult/child $78/28)* has been a top experience since the bridge was built in 1889. Once across, tree trails, wildlife and more bridges fill your day.

MAP P130 **D3**

**PLANNING TIP**
Buy bridge tickets in advance online. This helps you skip long queues, ensures entry on busy days, and often gives you access to special discounts.

### Treetops Adventure
Stop midway along the 140m-long suspension bridge to enjoy the mountain and river views, and snap photos if you can free a hand. In the park on the other side, **Treetops Adventure** thrills with a series of smaller suspension bridges dangling above Douglas-fir trees, some 1300 years old. For kids, the fun timber-frame treehouse – made using recycled and repurposed wood – is the best part.

### Cliffwalk
Keen to continue the sky-high thrills? Shimmy along the adrenaline-pumping **Cliffwalk**, a cantilevered walkway that clings to a granite cliff, about 30 stories high. Glass-floored viewing decks allow you look directly below your feet into the canyon – a heart-pounding, but safe, thrill.

### Birds of Prey
Get up close with a great horned owl or stand within arm's reach of a bald eagle at **Birds of Raptors Ridge**, an on-site educational facility committed to educating visitors on birds of prey such as owls, raptors and falcons. It's open weekends in April and May, daily June to September.

Scan this QR code for info, tickets and events.

⭐ **TOP EXPERIENCE**

# Grouse Mountain

This 'peak of Vancouver' is a mountain playground accessed by gondola (included in mountain admission). A top spot for winter skiing and snowboarding, the local hill is popular for summer hiking, biking and wildlife watching.

### Grouse Grizzly Bears

For an up-close look at Vancouver's resident birds and bears, ride the gondola up **Grouse Mountain** and check out daily educational demonstrations with owls, falcons and eagles at **Birds in Motion**. Stop by to observe Grinder and Coola, Grouse's rescued orphan grizzly bears.

### Mother Nature's Stairmaster

Reduce your mountain admission fee by hiking up the ultra-steep **Grouse Grind**, a 2.5km-long uphill 'grind' on foot, up many wooden and stone steps winding through dense forest. The footpath is one-way only, meaning you'll need to buy a $20 'download' gondola ticket to get back down.

### Alpine Action

In summer zoom down the mountain at speeds of up to 45km/hr on the **Grouse Gravity Coaster**. Or ride on a gondola rooftop with a **Skyride Surf Adventure**. Younger kids (3–8yrs) can run wild in **Kids Tree Canopy Adventure**, a treetop village of treehouses connected with cargo nets, wavy bridges, a curly slide and obstacle chimney. In winter, skiers and boarders cruise down 33 alpine ski runs, suitable for all skill levels.

MAP P130 **E1**

**PLANNING TIP**
May to September, free shuttle buses link Canada Place with Grouse Mountain's bottom gondola station (mountain admission ticket incl return gondola adult/child $82/42). Winter ski passes cost extra.

Scan this QR code for the complete lowdown on Grouse Mountain.

# Walk Lower Lonsdale

This loop through Lower Lonsdale takes you into the heart of North Vancouver's reinvented Shipyards District. Discover a once-gritty industrial zone, refreshed with oceanfront attractions, scenic boardwalk promenades and a full menu of tasty pit stops. Take your time – there's lots to do and discover.

| START | END | LENGTH |
|---|---|---|
| Lonsdale Quay | Burgoo Bistro | 1km; one hour |

### 1 Arrival Afloat

After sailing 15 minutes by SeaBus across the water from Vancouver's Waterfront Station, walk up the ramp at North Vancouver's **Lonsdale Quay** and turn right. Admire skyline views of Vancouver from the boardwalk. Sit and take it all in by the outdoor fountain before heading inside.

### 2 Market Meander

**Lonsdale Quay Market** *(lonsdalequay.com)* is lined with food stands and artisan stores; it even has an on-site microbrewery. A standout afternoon spot is the sun-filled patio of **King Taps Lonsdale Quay**, filling two floors of one corner of the market. On Wednesday afternoons, June to October, catch the **Coast Valley Farmers Market** *(coastvalleymarkets.com)* here.

### 3 Gallery Goods

A symbol of the area's revitalization, visit the striking **Polygon Gallery** *(thepolygon.ca)*. Check out the upper-floor gallery with views across to downtown Vancouver. Shop in the store for unique gifts, including locally handmade ceramics before heading to your next stop.

### 4 Historic Mural

At **Old Wallace Shipyards**, look for the large-format mural of the yesteryear shipyard site, showing hundreds of tough-as-nails men gearing up for work. The work is a collaborative art piece that showcases the area's redevelopment since it was first established in 1906.

### 5 Hidden Photo Stop

North Vancouver's most photographed alleyway, **Fun Alley**, was decorated in a kaleidoscope of color by artist Lukas Kasper, in collaboration with participating youth, in 2017. The street art project is the 10th installation by Studio in the City, an annual program by the City of North Vancouver offering youth the chance to apprentice in art in public spaces.

### 6 Designer Resales

Further north, **Hunter & Hare** *(hunterandhare.com)* is a classy women's consignment store offering a stylish selection of name-brand fashion finds at reasonable prices. It sells jewelry, accessories and home goods too. The bright, modern space is a great spot to pick up that perfect pair of jeans or cute keepsake for a friend.

### 7 Lunch Break

Conclude your day out with dinner at Burgoo Bistro (p138), a popular bistro-style restaurant where savory comfort foods are best enjoyed with an ice-cold pint of local beer. The SeaBus terminal, and a short hop back to downtown Vancouver, are just steps away.

## EXPERIENCES

### Wander Deep Cove Village    VILLAGE
MAP: ① P130 H3

It may be small but the waterfront village of **Deep Cove** (*deepcovebc.ca*) is a delightful spot to spend the day. The two-block strip leading to the water is lined with quaint cafes and locally owned shops. Once you hit the waterfront, you can choose to settle in for a picnic on the large grassy area, play on the towering play structure, sink your toes in the sandy beach and cool off with a dip in the ocean.

Or take to the water for some aquatic adventures. Deep Cove's sheltered waters make an ideal – and idyllic – spot for first-timers trying their hand at paddling. Lessons and tours are available at the **Deep Cove Kayak Centre** (*deepcovekayak.com; 2hrs single/double kayak $49/72*). Stand-up paddle boarding is another popular pick; an intro class costs $79.

### Hike Quarry Rock    HIKING
Steps from Deep Cove village is the trailhead for the popular **Quarry Rock** (MAP: ② P130 H3) hike, a stunning forested trail with wooden steps and gravel pathways that lead to beautiful views of **Burrard Inlet** from its final lookout point: a giant rock surface with panoramic views. The trail is well-maintained and easy to trek for all ages; dogs are welcome. Allow 1.5 to two hours (3.8km) round-trip. Back at base, grab a maple donut at **Honey Doughnuts & Goodies** (MAP: ③ P130 H3; *honeydoughnuts.com*), a local and celeb favorite.

### Shop the Shipyards District    SHOPPING
On North Vancouver's waterfront in Lower Lonsdale, **Shipyards District** (*theshipyardsdistrict.ca*) is the central activity hub for Vancouver's North Shore, home to the area's best festivals and events, and packed with restaurants, breweries, galleries and shops where you can buy everything from small-batch skincare products to locally roasted coffee and vintage-style fashion pieces. Easily accessible from downtown Vancouver by a short 15-minute passenger SeaBus, and serviced by a free shuttle in situ for getting around the area, it's easy to explore car-free.

### Head for the Hills    MOUNTAINS
Vancouver's North Shore is home to three local mountains, all within an hour from downtown Vancouver and favorite winter destinations for local Vancouverites; some offer all-season alpine adventures.

Grouse Mountain (p133) is the most visitor-friendly, with gondolas, a wildlife refuge and year-round attractions, including winter skiing and summer hiking. A 30-minute drive north from downtown Vancouver, **Cypress Mountain** (MAP: ④ P130 B1; *cypressmountain.com*) is lauded for having the largest, most varied terrain for more serious winter-sports enthusiasts. **Mt Seymour** (MAP: ❺ P130 **H2**; *mtseymour.ca)* meanwhile, a half-hour drive northeast from downtown, is a family-owned ski spot, with lots of powder and smaller crowds.

To get a handle on the thriving downhill mountain biking scene, check in with **North Shore Mountain Bike Association** *(nsmba.ca)*.

### Family Fun at Maplewood Farm  FARM
MAP: ❻ P130 **G4**

For kids who love animals, you'll find family fun at **Maplewood Farm** *(maplewoodfarm.bc.ca)*, a 2-hectare educational farm and petting zoo tucked in North Vancouver's Seymour neighborhood. The farm is home to 200 animals, including pigs, goats, sheep, chickens, rabbits, horses and cows. Picturesque trails weave around a shaded pond where you can feed ducks, and there's lots of picnic space if you want to settle in for a snack too.

### Cross the Bridge at Lynn Canyon Park  SUSPENSION BRIDGE

A lesser-known alternative to the more touristy Capilano Suspension Bridge, **Lynn Canyon Park** (MAP: ❼ P130 **G3**; *lynncanyon.ca)* has a suspension bridge that's equally as thrilling, teetering over trees 50m above the canyon floor. The bridge has been an attraction here since 1912, but unlike its more popular sister bridge, it's free to cross. You'll find a variety of hiking and walking trails on the other side that connect to nearby parks, including Lynn Headwaters, Rice Lake and Inter River Park. There are also scenic swimming holes if you want to take a dip. The park is home to the **Lynn Canyon Ecology Centre** (MAP: ❽ P130 **G3**; *ecologycentre.ca; free)*, where you can learn about its history through great visual displays, and pick up souvenirs at its shop.

### Stretch Your Legs At Lighthouse Park  PARK
MAP: ❾ P130 **A3**

Accessible via transit bus from downtown Vancouver, or if you're driving, turn left on Marine Dr after crossing the Lions Gate Bridge to reach **Lighthouse Park** *(lighthousepark.ca)*. Some of the region's oldest trees live within this accessible 75-hectare park, listed as a national historic site, including a rare stand of original coastal forest and plenty of gnarly, copper-trunked arbutus trees. About 13km of hiking trails crisscross the area, including a recommended trek that leads to the rocky perch of **Point Atkinson Lighthouse** – ideal for capturing camera-worthy shots of the Burrard Inlet.

## LISTINGS

# Best Places for...

**$** Budget  **$$** Midrange  **$$$** Top End

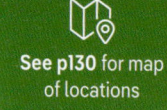

See p130 for map of locations

## Eating

### Casual Dining

**Nook $**
**10** H1

Cozy Italian eatery featuring house-made antipasto, pasta and wood-fired pizza using fresh, local ingredients. The standout dish is spaghetti bolognese – rich, comforting and perfectly crafted. *nookrestaurants. com; 11:30am-10pm*

**Burgoo Bistro $$**
**11** G1

With the feel of a cozy rustic cabin, complete with large stone fireplace, and a menu of international comfort dishes, Burgoo warms up the coolest of nights. Try beef bourguignon, grilled-cheese sandwiches or chicken-and-shrimp-packed farmers gumbo. *burgoo.ca; 11:30am-9pm Sun-Thu, to 10pm Fri & Sat*

**Anatoli Souvlaki $$**
**12** G1

This family-run Greek restaurant has been a Lonsdale strip staple since 1984, serving spanakopita and souvlaki long before the iconic Lonsdale Quay opened. A tiny patio is perfect for people-watching, and the cozy interior is warm and inviting. *thegreekby anatoli.com; 11:30am-10pm Tue-Thu, to 11pm Fri & Sat, to 9pm Mon*

**Cliff House Restaurant $$**
**13** D3

Enjoy great fish and chips washed down with local craft beer at this bistro-like eatery in the Capilano Suspension Bridge Park. Peruse photos of yesteryear Capilano on the walls, or perch on the patio in warm weather. *capbridge. com; 11am-5pm*

### Patios

**King Taps Lonsdale Quay $$**
**14** F2

Don't be fooled by its size: you'll likely have to wait for a seat at this packed two-level restaurant in Lonsdale Quay. With double-decker waterfront patios and a tasty menu featuring pizzas, pastas, burgers and bowls, the wait is worth it. *kingtaps.com; 11am-midnight Mon-Fri, from 10am Sat & Sun*

**Arms Reach Bistro $$**
**15** H3

Arms Reach Bistro perfectly balances upscale elegance and laid-back charm with its ambiance and menu. Dishes blend high-end touches like truffle oil and crème fraîche with cozy, playful fare like Angry Chicken and Rocket Spaghetti, best enjoyed on the picture-perfect patio. *armsreachbistro.com; noon-9pm, from 11am Sat & Sun*

**Beach House $$$**
**16** C3

In a 1912 heritage building, with West Coast–themed space and a spacious waterfront patio, this is a top spot in West Vancouver. Views of Howe Sound are sweeping. Pair jumbo lump crab cake with a glass of rose. *thebeachhouserestaurant.ca; 11am-11pm Mon-Fri, from 10am Sat & Sun*

### Fine Dining

**Pier 7** $$
 G2

Found in the heart of the Shipyard District, this boat-to-table seafood spot serves superb shucked oysters, salmon and crab. The seafood tower for two is a top choice, and if you don't like fish, it serves great burgers and steaks too. *pierseven.ca; hours vary*

**Observatory** $$$
⑱ E1

Make dinner special with a table at this restaurant on Grouse Mountain. Enjoy a multi-course meal and fine wine while taking in sweeping city views. *observatoryrestaurant.ca; 5-10pm*

**Sempre Uno** $$$
⑲ G1

Fine Italian dining with a menu that unites all the regions of Italy. Try a popular pasta dish like *taglierini all'aragosta* (lobster tagliolini) and save space for the decadent tiramisu. *sempreuno.com; 5-10pm Wed-Sat, to 9pm Sun*

# Drinking

### Breweries

**Troller Ale House**
⑳ A2

Troller Ale House in Horseshoe Bay made history in 1982 as Canada's first post-Prohibition pub to serve micro-brewed beer. Today, it remains a laid-back hangout, offering a wide selection of local brews. *trolleralehouse.com; 11am-11pm*

**Queen's Cross Pub**
㉑ E3

It's a hike up Lonsdale Ave from the SeaBus stop to this tradional-style, gable-roofed neighborhood pub. Formerly the kind of place where you had the choice of Bud or Molson, the pub now has a tasty commitment to regional craft brews. *queenscross.com; 11am-11pm Sun-Thu, to 1am Fri & Sat*

### Coffee

**Nemesis Coffee Polygon**
㉒ G1

Single-origin pour-overs, bold brunch dishes like bodega sando, and indulgent pastries – think tiramisu croissants – make this coffee address stand out. Located inside Dope Bakehouse at the Polygon Gallery, it's a fun fusion of cafe culture and art. *nemesis.coffee; 8am-4pm Mon-Fri, 9am-5pm Sat & Sun*

**United Strangers**
㉓ G3

This little family-owned coffee shop is worth a stop on your way to Deep Cove. Grab a great cup of coffee or a soft-serve cone, and browse the corner store inside while chatting with friendly locals. *unitedstrangerscoffee.com; 7:30am-5pm*

# Shopping

### Fashion & Accessories

**Unity Clothing**
㉔ H1

This locally owned clothing store, in the heart of Lower Lonsdale, is a community favorite where you can find everything from cute summer dresses to cozy knit sweaters. Browse fashionable accessories to complete your outfit. *unityclothing.ca; hours vary*

139

## ★ WORTH A TRIP

# Whistler

Two massive mountains, Whistler and Blackcomb, make up the world-renowned ski town known as Whistler – North America's largest ski resort, and arguably the best. But this isn't just a winter spot. Whistler offers hiking, biking, culture and cuisine worth visiting for any time of year.

**GETTING THERE**
Whistler is a scenic two-hour drive north of Vancouver by car, bus or shuttle. Seasonal seaplanes get you there in 35 minutes. In Whistler, public buses, seasonal free shuttles and 24-hour taxis get you around.

Scan this QR code for lift and terrain updates.

### Hit the Slopes

Offering a mix of thrilling terrain for advanced skiers (Olympians often train here) and scenic base hills for beginner boarders, **Whistler** is a true wonderland for snow-sports lovers of all levels. If snowshoeing is more your pace, ❶ **Whistler Olympic Park** *(whistlerolympicpark.com)* features over 30km of trails to explore – self-guided or with a guide. For adrenaline junkies, snowmobiling tours wind through Whistler's scenic back trails.

Host of the 2010 Winter Olympic and Paralympic Games and the main attraction to Whistler is ❶ **Blackcomb** (whistlerblackcomb.com). Skiers and snowboarders carve across the dual-mountain resort's snowy expanse from November to May (buy lift tickets in advance to save money). Come spring, ski runs transform into dusty trails where mountain bikers embrace gravity's pull as they ride, glide and fly like eagles, hopefully landing as gracefully. With 70 gravity-defying trails, ❸ **Whistler Mountain Bike Park** is world-renowned.

Connecting Whistler and Blackcomb is the colossal ❹ **Peak 2 Peak Gondola**, offering sweeping alpine views from the sky year-round. Summer reveals a network of hiking trails, plus the awe-inspiring ❺ **Cloudraker Skybridge** and

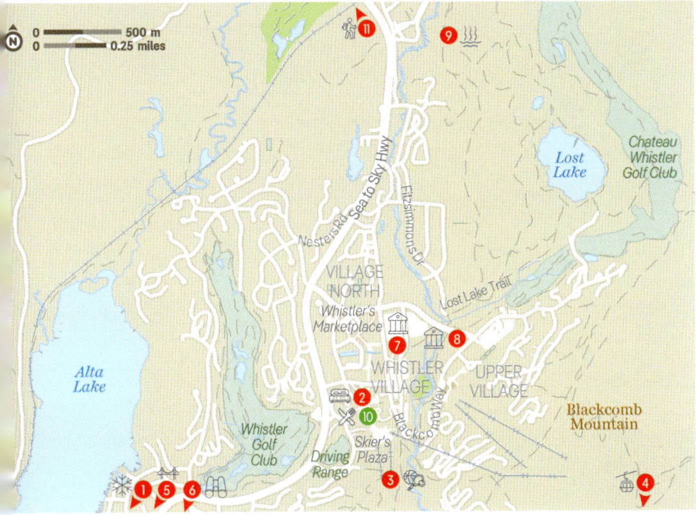

**6 Raven's Eye viewing platform**, both reachable via the Peak Chair. From the top, lift-accessed routes and panoramic views of glacial landscapes stretch in every direction. If you're planning to hike, be sure to plan ahead.

## Cultural Connector

Cycle or stroll along the self-guided **Cultural Connector** – a scenic, tree-lined pathway that leads you to six significant cultural sites. Whistler is a hub for arts and culture, featuring galleries that house some of the country's top works of art: The **7 Audain Art Museum** (audainartmuseum.com; adult/child $22/free) displays an Emily Carr masterpiece from 1912. At the **8 Squamish Lil'wat Cultural Centre** (slcc.ca; adult/child $25/12), historical stories, cultural works and immersive Indigenous cultural experiences

**PLANNING TIP**
Consider visiting Whistler during shoulder seasons (spring and fall) for better prices and smaller crowds. Year-round, book accommodation and activities in advance.

**QUICK BREAK**
Enjoy a glass of bubbly and a plate of charcuterie, or people-watch over a warming fondue or grilled cheese, on the tiny patio of ❿ **Flute & Fromage**.

showcase the traditional territories of two Nations that overlap in the Whistler region, the Squamish Nation and Lil'wat Nation.

## Mountain Nordic Spa

In a destination that is celebrated for its outdoor exploits, downtime is also desirable. At ❾ **Scandinave Spa** *(scandinave.com; admission $118, massages from $135)* you can enjoy the benefits of traditional Nordic-style hydrotherapy, with steams and soaks set in a West Coast wilderness setting. Silence is mandatory at this spa, where a cycle of hot-cold-rest-repeat takes you through eucalyptus steam rooms, outdoor hot baths, chilly Nordic waterfalls and cold plunge pools. Fireside resting spots and solariums inspire rest and

Blackcomb (p140)

relaxation. Wrap up your visit with a restorative, deep tissue or Swedish relaxation massage and you'll leave feeling totally refreshed.

## Illuminated Night Walk

When the sun sets, alpine adventures really begin. Step into the darkness of dimly-lit trails and enter a wilderness wonderland filled with songs, stories and incredible sights. The ⑪ **Vallea Lumina** *(vallealumina.com; adult/child $60/20)* multimedia night walk, which can be found just outside Whistler on Cougar Mountain, is part of a multi-city series created by Montreal-based Moment Factory. Stroll along illuminated trails, following the journey of a father-daughter duo – the legend of two long-ago hikers – and see what they discover in the depths of the forest. Through stunning visuals, soothing songs and curious clues, you'll uncover mysteries that surround you on a night journey like no other.

## Helicopter & Ice Cave Tour

For an unforgettable, ultra-luxe escape, fly over Canada's southernmost ice fields on an A-class helicopter and then explore a series of incredible ice caves by snowmobile, snow bike or snow buggy. The fully-guided, five-hour **Heli Sled & Ice Caves Tour** *(headlinemountainholidays.com; per person $1995),* run by Headline Mountain Holidays and departing from Whistler Heliport, will take your breath away as you navigate a labyrinth of aqua-blue ice caves while learning about the geological features of the grottos. Then sit in awe and enjoy a mountain-top artisan lunch while taking it all in. Explore an evolving landscape of ice flows, volcanic peaks, and wildlife that can only be accessed by air.

**FUNCTION JUNCTION**

A lesser-known Whistler neighborhood, Function Junction was originally an area filled with non-touristy commercial business and service sites. In recent years, the area has evolved into a creative hub, where you'll find art studios, coffee roasters, vintage shops, craft breweries and distilleries – even a small chocolate factory. It's also home to quirky activities like axe throwing and escape rooms.

# Vancouver Toolkit

| | |
|---|---|
| **Family Travel** | 146 |
| **Accommodations** | 147 |
| **Food, Drink & Nightlife** | 148 |
| **LGBTIQ+ Travelers** | 150 |
| **Health & Safe Travel** | 151 |
| **Responsible Travel** | 152 |
| **Accessible Travel** | 154 |
| **Nuts & Bolts** | 155 |

Gastown (p53)
ELENA ALEX FERNS/SHUTTERSTOCK

# Family Travel

Packed with green spaces, playgrounds, beaches and splash pads, as well as kid-centric attractions, free events and safe, walkable streets, Vancouver is one of Canada's top urban destinations for families.

### Stroller-Friendly City

From stroller-friendly mats that make it easy to push your pram along the sandy shores of the city's most popular beaches, to elevators, ramps and stable walkways at Vancouver's top attractions, you can see and do anything here with a stroller in tow.

### FAMILY-FRIENDLY PUBS

Kids can enter most Vancouver pubs with an adult, especially family-friendly or restaurant-style ones, but not the bar area. Most allow minors until 10pm, although rules vary – call ahead to confirm.

### Playgrounds, Parks & Pools

Packed with playgrounds, parks and outdoor pools, Vancouver is a dream destination for families. Stanley Park is speckled with wide-open parks, play spaces and splash pads, as well as Second Beach Pool, one of the city's only heated outdoor pools. There are over 160 playgrounds in Vancouver (many found right downtown), including Creekside Park (Vancouver's largest). For the best playgrounds, check out **Vancouver Playgrounds** (*vancouverplaygrounds.com*).

### Public Transportation

Whether you're taking a TransLink bus, SeaBus or SkyTrain, kids under 12 ride for free. On BC Ferries, children under five don't pay.

### Water Parks

Kids cool off in summer at free water parks, including North America's largest, on Granville Island.

### Baby Change Stations

Most museums, shopping centers, cafes and restaurants offer baby-changing facilities, with drop-down tables in unisex or women's washrooms.

ELNUR/SHUTTERSTOCK

# Accommodations

There are ample places to stay in Vancouver; most hotels are downtown. Airbnbs, B&Bs and hostels are affordable options.

## Where to Stay if You Love...

### Chic Shopping & Art
**Yaletown & Granville Island** (p69) These neighboring coastal communities combine chic shops with the artisan center of the city for the best of both worlds.

### Beaches & Boutiques
**Kitsilano & UBC** (p108) While there aren't any hotels directly in the area, a stay closer to Kits sets you up for beach days and boutique browsing.

### Hipster Vibes & Street Art
**Main Street & Mt Pleasant** (p85) Pick a hotel that's closer to Main Street if you love street art, vintage shops and Michelin dining.

### Outdoor Adventure
**North Shore** (p128) Gateway to ski hills, hiking and biking trails, and paddling coves. Stay in Shipyards District to be closest to the action.

### Bar Hopping & Nightlife
**Downtown & West End** (p33) For drinking and dancing at night, in the heart of the action, pick a place near Granville St or Davie St.

---

**OUR PICK**

**We Love to Stay in...**

**Downtown & West End** (p33) For the best of it all, stay near the waterfront in the downtown Coal Harbour area. From here, you can walk to top attractions like Stanley Park and Vancouver Art Gallery. Whale-watching tours and float planes are close by, and restaurants and bars are everywhere.

---

**HOW MUCH FOR A NIGHT IN A**

**Hostel dorm room** from $50

**Midrange room** from $150

**Four-star hotel room** from $300

# Food, Drink & Nightlife

### 🏥 Allergies & Intolerances

People with food allergies and intolerances generally won't have an issue while dining in Vancouver. Most restaurants are happy to accommodate special requests. Staff often even ask if you have any allergies or intolerances before you order. Many restaurants offer separate vegan, gluten-free and alcohol-free menu options.

Restaurants fill up quickly in Vancouver so you'll want to book ahead. Reservations can easily be made for most restaurants online by visiting opentable.ca.

---

## FOOD TRUCKS

Venture beyond the usual sit-down spots and try some of the city's best (and more diverse) dishes at a downtown food truck. **Japadog** *(japadog.com)*, usually set up downtown at the corner of Burrard St & Smithe St, is the city's most famous, known for its inventive Japanese-inspired hot dogs.

---

###  Ocean Wise

Vancouver is recognized for its sustainable seafood scene. When dining out, look for the Ocean Wise symbol on menus indicating dishes prepared using responsibly sourced seafood. The label is a local initiative set up by Vancouver Aquarium to promote ocean-friendly choices and protect marine life.

###  Pay the Bill

At sit-down restaurants, your bill won't be presented to you until you ask for it. For casual food counters, you might have to pay upon ordering; the food will be brought to your seat.

**Taxes** Expect to see additional taxes added to your bill, including a 5% federal Goods and Services Tax (GST) for meals and, in some cases, an additional 7% Provincial Sales Tax (PST) for alcohol and carbonated drinks, for a total of 12%.

**Tipping** Whether dining in or getting takeout, a tip on top of the bill total is common; 18% to 25% is standard.

**PRICE RANGES**

The average cost for a main course meal (excluding drinks) in Vancouver:
**$** less than $20
**$$** $20–35
**$$$** from $35

**OPENING HOURS**

**Coffee shops** 7am to 6pm (some close earlier)
**Restaurants** 10am to 10pm (some offer happy hour 2pm to 5pm)
**Fast-food outlets** 10am to midnight (hours vary)

 **Going Out**

**The scene**

Nightlife in Vancouver offers a good mix of cozy cocktail lounges, lively bars and nightclubs, and late-night eateries. Whether you're looking to settle into a dark corner for drinks and conversation, or dance the night away on a lively dancefloor, Vancouver has it all.

**When to go** The city starts to stir after 10pm, which is when you'll want to arrive to experience the best energy. Weekend nights are busiest, but midweek evenings – especially Thursdays – often offer the same buzzy atmosphere without the overwhelming crowds.

**At the door** While Vancouver's dress code isn't strict, showing up polished helps make a good impression. Carry two forms of ID, ideally with a photo, as proof of age is mandatory for entrance. Cash is still king for cover fees at smaller spots; so plan ahead to avoid any surprises.

FROM TOP LEFT: ETORRES/SHUTTERSTOCK, SERGIY KUZMIN/SHUTTERSTOCK

## HOW MUCH FOR A

**Food-court meal**
$10

**Pizza slice**
$4

**Happy-hour beer special**
$6

**Dinner for two in a neighborhood restaurant**
$45 (excluding drinks)

**Craft beer for two**
$18

**Fine-dining meal for two**
$100

**Cocktails for two**
$25

**TOOLKIT | FOOD, DRINK & NIGHTLIFE**

# LGBTIQ+ Travelers

Vancouver stands out as a friendly, secure place for LGBTIQ+ visitors, with great celebrations, heritage tours and queer bars.

## Gayborhoods

Vancouver's vibrant LGBTIQ+ scene is centered around a few key neighborhoods where LGBTIQ+ locals and visitors can feel safe, connected and celebrated.

**West End** Particularly the Davie Village area, is the heart of the city's queer culture, offering a diverse mix of bars, restaurants, shops and community spaces catering to LGBTQI+ people of all identities.

**Commercial Drive** Affectionately nicknamed 'The Drive', this strip has long been recognized for its strong lesbian community and inclusive vibe. Cozy cafes and cultural spots celebrate diversity.

**Mount Pleasant** has emerged as a creative and inclusive neighborhood, popular with younger queer residents. It features artsy venues and indie shops.

### OUR PICKS

**Events By Month**

**January/February** PuSh International Performing Arts Festival

**March** Vancouver International Burlesque Festival

**July** Pride Run & Walk, Burnaby Pride Festival, Summer Sounds Pride Celebration, Cirque du Slay, Normie Pride Fest

**August** Vancouver Pride Parade, Davie Village Pride Festival, Vancouver Trans March

**September** Vancouver Queer Film Festival

### XTRA XTRA!

Check out **Xtra Vancouver** (xtramagazine.com), an online magazine and community platform covering LGBTIQ+ culture, politics and health.

### QUEER HISTORY WALKING TOUR

Discover Vancouver's queer history on a walking tour celebrating drag kings, Two-Spirit leaders, trans-activists and queer pioneers.

## Resources

• **qmunity.ca** Comprehensive online portal of BC's queer, trans and Two-Spirit resource center, providing a safe space for self-expression. • **whatsonqueerbc.com** Website listing LGBTIQ+ resources, events, shops and services, including support groups.

# Health & Safe Travel

Vancouver is generally safe, but like anywhere, practice safety precautions as you navigate your way around.

###  WATCH FOR WILDLIFE

Black bears, cougars and coyotes are occasionally spotted in busy city parks. Raccoons, squirrels and Canadian geese are regularly seen; give them space – they're not friendly. If you encounter wildlife, keep your distance, stay calm, don't feed them and back away slowly.

### Weather Awareness

Vancouver's coastal climate is unpredictable. Sunshine can quickly turn to rain or fog, especially in the mountains or forests. Always dress in layers and carry essentials like water, a map and a fully charged phone when exploring outdoors to avoid risks like hypothermia or getting lost. Despite the mild temperatures, UV exposure can still be strong even on cloudy days or near water, so don't forget sunscreen when heading out on any adventure.

###  Drinking & Driving

The legal blood-alcohol limit is 0.08%. You can face serious penalties even at 0.05%.

### Bike Lanes

Vancouver is bike-friendly, with dedicated lanes designated for bikes all around town. In downtown and along the seawall, avoid standing or walking in clearly marked cycling paths. When driving, yield to bikes, stay mindful of their marked routes (especially at intersections) and always check for cyclists before turning or opening your car door when stationary.

--- **CANNABIS** ---

Cannabis, consumed in private or designated areas, is legal for anyone 19 years or older. Public consumption and driving impaired are illegal and strictly enforced.

## QUICK INFO

### Security
Avoid roaming the Downtown Eastside area at night; keep valuables hidden.

### Privacy
Don't film people without consent, especially in public spaces.

### Tap Water
Vancouver's tap water is clean and perfectly fine to drink.

# Responsible Travel

Support local businesses, choose sustainable venues and give back to Indigenous communities. Enjoy authentic experiences.

### Support Local
Skip the chain stores and venture beyond the more touristy attractions. Consider a local-led walking tour to learn about the city's hidden spots and secrets. Try the Gastronomic Gastown tour by **Vancouver Foodie Tours** *(foodietours.ca)* or the Indigenous-owned Talking Trees tour through Stanley Park by **Talaysay Tours** *(talaysay.com)*. Dine at Indigenous restaurant Salmon n' Bannock (p105).

### Choose Sustainable Venues
Stay at eco-friendly hotels with green certifications, like the Fairmont Waterfront or Shangri-La, which support sustainable tourism efforts while protecting the planet.

### OUR PICK
**Meaningful Stay**
**Skwachàys Lodge** *(skwachays.com)* is Indigenous-owned, offering authentic art and housing support for local Indigenous communities, making your stay meaningful and impactful.

### Leave a Small Footprint
Use reusable water bottles and mugs, walk, cycle or take public transit to reduce emissions, and choose eco-friendly activities. Shop at resale stores and local boutiques to support sustainable fashion and small businesses. Practice 'leave no trace' by taking your garbage with you and leaving natural spaces as you find them.

### Resources
- **greekey.global** List of Vancouver's certified sustainable hotels
- **mobibikes.ca** Pay-per-day bike use
- **eco-meter.ca** Sustainable dining

## GIVE BACK

Support Indigenous communities by purchasing products from Indigenous-owned shops or the Bill Reid Gallery (p49) gift shop, where your dollars help support local makers and cultural preservation. Dine at Anh & Chi (p92), Vancouver's Vietnamese restaurant with a reservation-by-donation system, donating to local charities, blending delicious meals with meaningful giving.

### Get Hands-On

Vancouver offers a variety of volunteer opportunities that allow visitors to connect with local communities while making a lasting impact. Join beach cleanups organized by Vancouver Aquarium's **Ocean Wise** *(ocean.org/action/join-a-shoreline-cleanup)* to help protect the city's shoreline and marine life.

For an urban-farming experience, check **Sole Food Farms**, a social enterprise that has transformed a vacant lot into a productive garden providing fresh produce for the community and local restaurants, and jobs for those in need; see @solefoodfarms on Instagram for volunteer drop-in days.

### FARMERS MARKETS

Visit Vancouver's farmers markets to support local farmers and reduce your environmental footprint. Enjoy fresh, seasonal produce, handmade goods and connect directly with locals. Scan this QR code for locations.

### Climate Change & Travel

It's impossible to ignore the impact we have when traveling; Lonely Planet urges all travelers to engage with their travel carbon footprint, which will mainly come from air travel. While there often isn't an alternative, travelers can look to minimize the number of flights they take, opt for newer aircrafts and use cleaner ground transport, such as trains. One proposed solution – purchasing carbon offsets – unfortunately does not cancel out the impact of individual flights. While most destinations will depend on air travel for the foreseeable future, for now, pursuing ground-based travel where possible is the best course of action.

The **UN Carbon Offset Calculator** shows how flying impacts a household's emissions.

The **ICAO's carbon emissions calculator** allows visitors to analyse the $CO_2$ generated by point-to-point journeys.

# Accessible Travel

### Taxis & Rideshare
On your arrival at the airport, vehicle-rental companies can provide prearranged cars with hand controls. Accessible cabs are widely available at the airport and throughout the city, on request. Uber and Lyft offer wheelchair-accessible vehicles (WAV) – Uber through the WAV option in the app, and Lyft as a 'wheelchair' ride type (limited availability).

### Public Transportation
All TransLink SkyTrain, SeaBus and transit bus services are wheelchair accessible. Check the **TransLink** (translink.ca) website for a wide range of information on accessible transportation options around the region.

> **OUR PICK**
>
> **Vancouver Aquarium** (p44) offers a range of accessibility offerings. Throughout you'll find accessible pathways, elevators and wheelchair-friendly viewing platforms. For guests with sensory sensitivities, there are sensory-friendly hours, support staff and sensory kits with items like noise-canceling headphones available on loan. Mobility aids are available. The aquarium provides discounted admission for visitors with accessibility needs.

### ACCESSIBLE BEACHES
One of Vancouver's most popular beaches – Kitsilano Beach (p118) – has accessible beach mats and floating water wheelchairs, allowing those with mobility challenges to comfortably enjoy a beach day.

### Service Dogs
Visitors traveling with service dogs in Vancouver are legally allowed to bring them into restaurants, hotels and other businesses around the city – it's the law under BC's Guide Dog & Service Dog Act.

### CITY STREETS & SIGHTS
Almost all of Vancouver's city sidewalks have sloping ramps and crosswalks have audible signals. Most public buildings and attractions are wheelchair-accessible, equipped with ramps and elevators.

### Resources
- **vancouver.ca/accessibility** The City of Vancouver's dedicated website has plenty more information and resources about accessibility in the city.

# Nuts & Bolts

## Opening Hours

Most business hours are consistent throughout the year, with the exception of attractions, which often reduce their hours outside summer.

**Banks** 9am to 5pm weekdays; some open Saturday mornings.

**Shops** 10am to 6pm Monday to Saturday; noon to 5pm Sunday.

**Restaurants** 11:30am to 3pm and 5pm to 10pm.

**Coffee shops and cafes** From 8am, some earlier.

**Pubs and bars** Pubs open from 11:30am; bars often open from 5pm. They close at midnight or later.

### QUICK INFO

**Time zone** Pacific Standard Time

**City calling code** 604; also 778, 236, 672

**Emergency number** 911

**Population** 687,933 (Metro Vancouver 2,750,966)

## Tap Water

Vancouver's tap water is clean, fresh and safe to drink. It comes from protected mountain sources and is tested regularly. Most locals drink tap water instead of buying bottled water.

## Public Holidays

On national public holidays, transportation, museums and other services often operate on Sunday schedules. Holidays falling on weekends are usually observed the following Monday.

Major public holidays in Vancouver:

**New Year's Day** January 1

**Family Day** Third Monday in February

**Good Friday and Easter Monday** Late March to mid-April

**Victoria Day** Third Monday in May

**Canada Day** July 1

**BC Day** First Monday in August

**Labour Day** First Monday in September

**Thanksgiving** Second Monday in October

**Remembrance Day** November 11

**Christmas Day** December 25

**Boxing Day** December 26

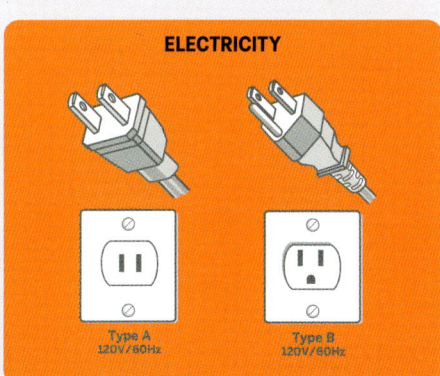

**ELECTRICITY**

Type A
120V/60Hz

Type B
120V/60Hz

# Index

Sights p000   Map pages p000

See also separate subindexes for:
- **Eating p158**
- **Drinking p159**
- **Shopping p159**

## A
accessible travel 154
accommodations 147
**Arbutus Greenway 118**
art 11, 28, 80
Audain Art Museum 141

## B
**BC Place Stadium 78**
**BC Sports Hall of Fame & Museum 78-9**
beaches 37-8
**Beaty Biodiversity Museum 115**
bicycle travel 26, 151
**Bill Reid Gallery of Northwest Coast Art 44**
bird-watching 74
**Blackcomb 140**
**Bloedel Conservatory 104**
boat travel 25, 26
boat trips 14
budget 21, 27, 147, 149
bus travel 25
business hours 149, 155

## C
**Canada Place 44**
**Canadian Trail 43**
cannabis 20, 151
**Capilano Suspension Bridge 132**
car travel 24, 25-6
children, travel with 15, 146
**Chinatown 53-67, 54**
  drinking 66-7
  experiences 60-3
  food 64-6
  shopping 67
  top experiences 55-6
  transportation 53
  walking tour 58-9, **58**
**Chinatown Gate 59**
**Chinatown Millennium Gate 59**
**Chinatown Storytelling Centre 59, 60**
**Chinese-Canadian Museum 62-3**
**Christ Church Cathedral 43**
climate 22
climate change 153
**Convention Centre West Building 43**
costs 21, 27, 147, 149
**Creekside Park 90**
cruises 24
cultural festivals
  Dragon Boat Festival 22
  Eastside Culture Crawl 63
  Khatsahlano Street Party 119
  Powell Street Festival 61
  Vancouver International Children's Festival 22
  Vancouver International Jazz Festival 22
culture 12
currency 21
cycling, see bicycle travel
**Cypress Mountain 136-7**

## D
**David Lam Park 80**
**Deep Cove 136**
disabilities, travelers with 154
**Dominion Building 63**
**Downtown 33-49, 34-5**
  drinking 48-9
  experiences 44-5
  food 46-8
  shopping 49
  top experiences 36-41
  transportation 33
  walking tour 42-3, **42**
Downtown Eastside 45
drinking 149
**Dr Sun Yat-Sen Classical Chinese Garden 56-7, 59**

## E
electricity 155
**Engine 374 Pavilion 78**
etiquette 20
events, see festivals & events

## F
**Fairmont Hotel Vancouver 43**
**Fairview 97-107, 98-9**
  drinking 106-7
  experiences 104
  food 105-6
  shopping 107
  top experiences 100-1
  transportation 97
family travel 15, 146
festivals & events 22-3, 150
**Firehall Arts Centre 60**
**Flack Block 63**
food 9, 148-9
free attractions 15
**Fun Alley 135**
**Function Junction 143**

## G
**Gaoler's Mews 63**
**Gastown 53-67, 54**
  drinking 66-7
  experiences 60-3
  food 64-6
  shopping 67
  top experiences 57
  transportation 53
**Gastown Steam Clock 57**
gay travelers 150
**Granville Island 69-83, 70-1**
  drinking 82
  experiences 78-80
  food 81-2
  shopping 83
  top experiences 72-5
  transportation 69
  walking tour 76-7, **76**

156

Granville Island Public Market 72-5, 77
Granville Island Stage 80
Granville Island Water Park 79-80
Greenheart TreeWalk 115, 116
Grouse Mountain 133
Gulf of Georgia Cannery 127

### H
health 151
Heli Sled & Ice Caves Tour 143
Heritage Hall 91
highlights 6-15
Hogan's Alley Tours 61-2
Hotel Europe 63
HR MacMillan Space Centre 117

### I
Improv Centre, the 80
Indigenous cultures 12, 29, 89, 141-2
itineraries 16-19

### J
Jericho Beach 118

### K
Khatsahlano Street Party 119
Kids Market 78
Kitsilano 109-23, **110-11**
 drinking 121-2
 experiences 116-19
 food 120-1
 shopping 122-3
 transportation 109
Kitsilano Beach 118
Kitsilano Pool 117

### L
language 29
LGBTIQ+ travelers 150
Lighthouse Park 137
Little Italy 91
Lonsdale Quay 135
Lynn Canyon Ecology Centre 137
Lynn Canyon Park 137

### M
Main St 85-95, **86**
 drinking 93-4
 experiences 90-1
 food 92-3
 shopping 94-5

top experiences 87
transportation 85
walking tour 88-9, **88**
Malkin Bowl 44
Maple Tree Square 63
Maplewood Farm 137
marijuana 20, 151
Marine Building 43, 45
Marpole Museum & Historical Society 118
money 21
Morris & Helen Belkin Art Gallery 115, 117
Mt Pleasant 85
Mt Seymour 137
murals 88-9
Museum of Anthropology 112-13
Museum of Vancouver 116-17
museums & galleries 11, 12, *see also individual museums & galleries*

### N
Nat Bailey Stadium 104
nightlife 149
Nitobe Memorial Garden 115
North Shore 129-39, **130-1**
 drinking 139
 experiences 136-7
 food 138-9
 shopping 139
 top experiences 132-3
 transportation 129
 walking tour 134-5, **134**

### O
Old Wallace Shipyards 135
Olympic Cauldron 43
Olympic Village 90
opening hours 149, 155
Oppenheimer Park 61
outdoor activities 6, 132-3, 136-7, 140

### P
parks & gardens 8, 29
Paueru-gai 61
Peak 2 Peak Gondola 140-1
planning 20-1
Point Atkinson Lighthouse 137
Polygon Gallery 135
Port of Vancouver Discovery Centre 44
Pride Parade 22

Prospect Point 38
public holidays 155
public transportation 26-7

### Q
Quarry Rock 136
Queen Elizabeth Park 104

### R
Rail Workers Memorial 59
Railspur Alley 79
responsible travel 152-3
Richmond 124-7, **125**
Richmond Night Market 124-5
Rickshaw Theatre 60
Roundhouse Community Arts & Recreation Centre 78

### S
safe travel 151
Scandinave Spa 142-3
Science World 87
Shipyards District 136
skiing 140
snowboarding 140
South Granville 97-107, **98-9**
 drinking 106-7
 experiences 104
 food 105-6
 shopping 107
 top experiences 100-1
 transportation 97
 walking tour 102-3, **102**
Spanish Banks Beach 118
Squamish Lil'wat Cultural Centre 141-2
Stanley Park 36-9
Stanley Theatre 103, 104
Steveston Village 125-6
street art 88-9
sustainability 152

### T
taxis 24, 26
time 21
tipping 21
train travel 24, 25
transportation 24, 25-7
travel seasons 22, 23

### U
UBC 109-23, **110-11**
 drinking 121-2
 experiences 116-19

UBC *continued*
  food 120-1
  shopping 122-3
  top experiences 112-13
  transportation 109
  walking tour 114-15, **114-15**
UBC Asian Centre 115
UBC Botanical Garden 115, 116

**V**
Vallea Lumina 143
Vancouver Aquarium 44-5
Vancouver Art Gallery 40-1, 43
Vancouver Maritime Museum 116
Vancouver Police Museum & Archives 59, 61
Vancouver Public Library 43
VanDusen Botanical Garden 100-1
Vanier Park 119
volunteering 153

**W**
walking tours
  Chinatown 58-9, **58**
  Downtown 42-3, **42**
  Granville Island 76-7, **76**
  Main St 88-9, **88**
  North Shore 134-5, **134**
  South Granville 102-3, **102**
  UBC 114-15, **114**
water, drinking 151, 155
Waterfront Theatre 80
weather 22
weights & measures 20
West End 33-49, **34-5**
  drinking 48-9
  experiences 44-5
  food 46-8
  shopping 49
  top experiences 36-41
  transportation 33
whales 50-1
whale-watching 50-1
Whistler 140-3, **141**
Whistler Mountain Bike Park 140
Whistler Olympic Park 140
wildlife 74
wildlife 14, 50-1, 74, 100, 132, 151
Wreck Beach 115, 118

Yaletown 69-83, **70-1**
  drinking 82
  experiences 78-80
  food 81-2
  shopping 83
  transportation 69

Eating

Acorn 92
Acquafarina 47
Alimentaria Mexicana 73, 81
Anatoli Souvlaki 138
Anh & Chi 92
AnnaLena 121
Arms Reach Bistro 138
Bao Bei 65
Beach House 138-9
Birds & the Beets 65
Blue Water Cafe 81
Bon Macaron Patisserie 79
Botanist 47
Boulevard Kitchen & Oyster Bar 47
Bread Affair, A 81-2
Burdock & Co 90, 92
Burgoo Bistro 92, 135, 138
Cafe Medina 47
Chambar 47
Chinatown BBQ 56, 59
Cliff House Restaurant 138
DD Mau 64
Dockside Restaurant 81
Dumpling Trail 127
East is East 92
El Camino's 93
Elisa 60, 82
Fable Kitchen 120-1
Fanny Bay Oyster Bar & Shellfish Market 46
Fat Mao 64
Five Sails Restaurant 48
Flute & Fromage 142
Garden Cafe 101
Go Fish 81
Good Thief 93
Granville Island Licorice Parlour 77
Hawksworth 47

Heritage Asian Eatery 46
Honey Doughnuts & Goodies 136
Hunnybee Bruncheonette 64
Jam Cafe 46-7
Jam Cafe Kitsilano 120
Jamjar Canteen 120
Japadog 46
King Taps Lonsdale Quay 138
Kissa Tanto 65
L'Abattoir 65
Le Crocodile 47
Lee's Donuts 72, 77
Lila 93
Maenam 121
Mazarin 103
Meat & Bread 46, 64
MeeT in Gastown 65
Naam 120
Nero Belgian Waffle Bar 46
Nook 138
Nuba 65
Observatory 139
Paul's Omelettery 103
Peaked Pies 46
Phnom Penh 60, 64
Pier 7 139
Public Market Food Court 75
Published on Main 92
Ramen Butcher 64
Ramen Danbo 120
Rodney's Oyster House 82
Sandbar 81
Say Hey Cafe 64
Sempre Uno 139
SImpatico Ristorante 120
Sophie's Cosmic Cafe 120
St Lawrence Restaurant 65
Sula Indian Restaurant 92
Suyo Modern Peruvian 92
Tacofino 46
Tacofino Ocho 93
Tacofino Taco Bar 65
Tap & Barrel Bridges 81
Teahouse in Stanley Park 37, 47
Their There 120
Torafuku 60
Twisted Fork Bistro 47
Virtuous Pie 66
Water St Cafe 65
Wildlight Kitchen + Bar 121
Yasma 46
Zarak by Afghan Kitchen 93

# Drinking

33 Acres Brewing Company 94
49th Parallel Coffee 121
49th Parallel Coffee Roasters 94
Alibi Room 66
Aperture Coffee Bar 94
Artisan Sake Maker 77, 82
Bimini's Public House 121
Botanist 48
Brassneck Brewery 94
Brewhall 94
Caffè Artigiano 48
Caffè Mira 48-9
Delany's Coffee House 48
Electric Bicycle Brewing 94
Elysian Coffee 122
Flute & Fromage 142
Fountainhead Pub 48
Gallery Bistro 41
Galley Patio & Grill 121
Granville Island Brewing 77
Granville Island Brewing Taproom 82
Guilt & Co 66
Keefer Bar 66
Key Party 93
King Taps Lonsdale Quay 135
Koerner's Pub 113, 121
Laowai 66
Liberty Distillery 82
Lift Bar & Grill 48
Main St Brewing 93-4
Matchstick 82
Matchstick Coffee 94
Narrow Lounge 93
Nemesis Coffee 66-7
Nemesis Coffee Polygon 139
O5 Teas Rare Tea Bar 122
Off the Tracks 82
Pallet Coffee Roasters 122
Pumpjack Pub 48
Queen's Cross Pub 139
Revolver 66
Shameful Tiki Room 93
Silk Road Tea 122
Sing Sing Beer Bar 93
Six Acres 66
Small Victory 82, 103
Stanley's Bar & Grill 48
Steamworks Brew Pub 66
Tap & Barrel Bridges 51
Timbertrain Coffee 67
Troller Ale House 139
United Strangers 139
Uva Wine & Cocktail Bar 48
Wolf & Hound 121

# Shopping

Allison Wonderland Atelier 83
Arc'teryx 123
Bacci's 103, 107
Banyen Books & Sound 123
Beadworks 77
Beat Street Records 49
Bill Reid Gallery Shop 49
Book Warehouse 107
Community Thrift & Vintage Frock Shoppe 67
Cross Decor & Design 83
F as in Frank 95
Fine Finds 83
Front & Company 95
Geza Burghardt Luthiery 79
Golden Age Collectables 49
Gore St Vintage 67
Granville Island Broom Company 79
Granville Island Hat Shop 73
Granville Island Licorice Parlour 83
Granville Island Public Market 72-5, 77
Herschel Supply Co 67
Hunter & Hare 135
Ian Tan Art Gallery 107
John Fluevog Shoes 67
Kasama Chocolates 77, 83
Kidsbooks 122-3
Kids Market 77, 78
Kitsilano Farmers Market 122
Koko Monk 122
Kool Thing Vintage 62
Little Sister's Book & Art Emporium 49
Lonsdale Quay Market 135
Lucky's Books & Comics 95
Macleod's Books 49
Massy Books 67
Meinhardt Fine Foods 103, 107
Melanie Auld 123
Mink Chocolates 49
Mintage Mall 95
Mt Pleasant Farmers Market 91
Neptoon Records 94-5
Old Faithful 123
Opus Art Supplies 79, 83
Pacific Arts Market 103, 107
Pacific Boarder 123
Paper Hound 49
Paper-Ya 77, 83
Poppy Barley 123
Portobello West 83
Purdy's Chocolates 103, 107
Red Cat Records 94
Regional Assembly of Text 95
Richmond Night Market 124
Robson Street 45
Shayelily Jewelry 67
Silk Weaving Studio 83
Thomas Haas 122
Turnabout Luxury Resale 95
Unity Clothing 139
Urban Source 95
Vancouver Art Gallery Store 49
Vancouver Pen Shop 49
Vinyl Records 67
Walrus 107
West 4th Avenue 118
Zulu Records 123

# Send Us Your Feedback

We love to hear from travelers – your comments help make our books better. We read every word, and we guarantee that your feedback goes straight to the authors. Visit lonelyplanet.com/contact to submit your updates and suggestions.

Note: We may edit, reproduce and incorporate your comments in Lonely Planet products such as guidebooks, websites and digital products, so let us know if you are happy to have your name acknowledged. For a copy of our privacy policy visit lonelyplanet.com/legal.

### Acknowledgements

Cover photograph: Vancouver skyline, seen from Granville Island. Margitta Hild/4Corners

Back photograph: Grouse Mountain (p133). LeonWang/Shutterstock

## THIS BOOK

The 6th edition of Lonely Planet's Vancouver guidebook was researched and written by Bianca Bujan., who also wrote the previous edition. This guidebook was produced by the following:

**Destination Editor**
Jessica Lockhart

**Coordinating Editor**
Nicola Williams

**Cartographer**
Hunor Csutoros

**Production Editor**
Joel Cotterell

**Image Editor**
Maïa Booker

**Assisting Editors**
Katie Connolly, Melanie Dankel

**Cover Researcher**
Daisy Korpics

**Thanks to**
Fergal Condon, Gwen Cotter, Alison Kililea, Darren O'Connell

Although the authors and Lonely Planet have taken all reasonable care in preparing this book, we make no warranty about the accuracy or completeness of its content and, to the maximum extent permitted, disclaim all liability arising from its use.

All rights reserved. No part of this publication may be copied, stored in a retrieval system, or transmitted in any form by any means, electronic, mechanical, recording or otherwise, except brief extracts for the purpose of review, and no part of this publication may be sold or hired, without the written permission of the publisher. Lonely Planet and the Lonely Planet logo are trademarks of Lonely Planet and are registered in the US Patent and Trademark Office and in other countries. Lonely Planet does not allow its name or logo to be appropriated by commercial establishments, such as retailers, restaurants or hotels. Please let us know of any misuses: lonelyplanet.com/legal/intellectual-property.

Paper in this book is certified against the Forest Stewardship Council™ standards. FSC™ promotes environmentally responsible, socially beneficial and economically viable management of the world's forests.

Published by Lonely Planet Global Limited
CRN 554153
6th edition – May 2026
ISBN 978 1 83869 926 0
© Lonely Planet 2026
10 9 8 7 6 5 4 3 2 1
Printed in China